First Steps in Bonds

FINANCIAL TIMES

Prentice Hall

In an increasingly competitive world, it is quality
of thinking that gives an edge. An idea that opens new
doors, a technique that solves a problem, or an insight
that simply helps make sense of it all.

We work with leading authors in the fields of
management and finance to bring cutting-edge thinking
and best learning practice to a global market.

Under a range of leading imprints, including
Financial Times Prentice Hall, we create world-class
print publications and electronic products giving readers
knowledge and understanding which can then be
applied, whether studying or at work.

To find out more about our business and professional
products, you can visit us at www.business-minds.com

For other Pearson Education publications, visit
www.pearsoned-ema.com

Pearson
Education

First Steps in Bonds

*Successful Strategies without
the Rocket Science*

Peter Temple

FINANCIAL TIMES
Prentice Hall

An imprint of **Pearson Education**

Boston • San Francisco • New York • Toronto • Montreal • London • Munich
Paris • Madrid • Capetown • Sydney • Tokyo • Singapore • Mexico City

PEARSON EDUCATION LIMITED

Head Office:
Edinburgh Gate
Harlow CM20 2JE
Tel: +44 (0)1279 623623
Fax: +44 (0)1279 431059

London Office:
128 Long Acre, London WC2E 9AN
Tel: +44 (0)20 7447 2000
Fax: +44 (0)20 7240 5771
Website: www.financialminds.com

First published in Great Britain in 2002

ISBN: 0 273 65657 0

British Library Cataloguing in Publication Data
A CIP catalogue record for this book can be obtained from the British Library.

10 9 8 7 6 5 4 3 2 1

Designed by designdeluxe, Bath
Typeset by Land & Unwin (Data Sciences) Ltd, Northampton
Printed and bound in Great Britain by Bell & Bain Ltd, Glasgow

The Publishers' policy is to use paper manufactured from sustainable forests.

About the author

P eter Temple was born in West Yorkshire and is a graduate of the University of Wales, a former member of the London Stock Exchange, and a Fellow of the Securities Institute. He spent the first 18 years of his working life in fund management and investment banking, turning to full-time writing in 1988.

His articles cover a wide variety of investing topics and appear regularly in the *Financial Times*, *Investors Chronicle*, *Shares*, *International Fund Investment*, and in a number of other publications and financial websites. He has written several other books on investing, covering topics such as online investing, venture capital and hedge funds, including *First Steps in Shares* (2001, Financial Times Prentice Hall).

He and his wife live in Woodford Green, Essex, and have two grown-up children.

Contents

Acknowledgements

Writing a book for private investors about the bond markets has been something of a gleam in this eye of mine for some time. The finished product would not have appeared but for the help of a wide range of people.

Throughout, Jonathan Agbenyega at Pearson Education has been an enthusiastic supporter of the book, and my quest to produce something that would enable private investors to cut through the seeming complexity of the market and see through the fog with which some bond market operators seek to surround it.

Several industry insiders deserve special mention for giving their unstinting help, providing information on demand, and in some cases viewing early drafts of the manuscript. Thanks, in no particular order, go to: Tony DiLorenzo and Ian Phipps at Winterflood Securities, Mark Reynolds and Nick Bruell at Insinger Townsley, Tim Dickenson and colleagues at ISMA, the authors of the Barclays Capital Gilt Equity study, and David Frohiep at Moodys, all of whom had specific input into the book.

Over the years I have had cause to thank the following for enlarging my knowledge of the bond market in its various guises: Helena Morrissey at Newton Fund Managers, Paul Reed at Aberdeen Asset Management, Peter Warren at Goldman Sachs, and former colleagues like Manny Lloyd, Michael Noakes, AndreVan't Hoff, Barry Conway and others too numerous to mention.

David Kauders and Martin Bloomberg both read the entire manuscript and made numerous corrections and improvements. Penelope Allport conducted her usual efficient shepherding of the project through to publication.

Finally, closer to home, Lynn Temple did some of the writing and much of the research for the web-based material in Chapters 9 and 10 and created the database used to generate tables for these chapters. My son-in-law Matthew Creer read the entire manuscript from a lay person's standpoint and suggested a number of improvements, all of which have increased the clarity of the finished product.

It only remains to say that any errors and omissions which remain are entirely my responsibility.

Introduction

Most investors just buy shares in companies. Sometimes they make profits in doing so. In the long term, profits from share investing are often better than any other alternative. Many, however, can't or don't invest for the long term, or want something different from their investments than long-term capital growth. If you just invest over short periods, as the events of the past couple of years have shown, it's possible to buy shares and lose money very easily. Many shares offer little or no regular income.

This is where bonds come in. Bonds are IOUs issued by governments and companies and traded in a market like shares. They can offer a good regular return with less risk than shares. You get a predictable flow of interest payments once or twice a year, and your investment back in full when the bond matures.

Bond jargon – yields, spreads, credit ratings and basis points – is increasingly creeping into financial news broadcasts. But how do bonds work? Are they simply a safer, more boring alternative to stocks? Do they simply offer lower but more predictable returns? How do you value them? If you want to invest in bonds, how do you go about it? What type of bond should you buy?

> **How do bonds work? Are they simply a safer, more boring alternative to stocks?**

Thirty-two years ago I started my first job. On my first day in the investment department of a large insurance company, I got a crash course on the bond market. Having left university with solid 2.1 degree in economics, I was pretty cocky. The manager assigned to ease me into the job started explaining the intricacies of bond yields. For good measure, he lent me a textbook he was using for his actuarial exams. In short order, and despite a reasonable facility with numbers, I was lost. Soon, however, I was calculating yields on complex Canadian government bonds as though I had been doing it all my life.

Though the intricacies of bond market mathematics can be complicated, financial calculators handle them comfortably. Only normal numeracy is required. You need only understand the broad principles rather than the intricate algebra. The principles behind bond investing are essentially straightforward. Often they deal with putting numbers to simple ideas. How much would you pay to have money now rather than in a year's time? How much is that same amount worth to you two years from now? What is the probability that this or that company might go bust? What is a reasonable rate of return on your money? What are the likely future trends in inflation and interest rates?

I've wanted to write a book about bonds for a long time. Not a dry text-book, but one that brings the ideas behind the bond market to a wider readership; a book that looks at how to value bonds and at the practical aspects of investing in them. There are several reasons why I feel the time is right for a book that introduces bonds to a broader investing public.

One is that uncertain and volatile stock markets make many investors more cautious. After losses on technology shares, some investors are open to ideas about using other types of investment to reduce the risks they are running. Bonds are not risk free, but most are by no means as volatile as dot.coms or mobile phone companies.

Second, many professional investors routinely use bonds. Often they are employed as the core constituent of a diversified portfolio. So it is only prudent for longer term do-it-yourself investors to do the same – or at least to find out more about bond investing.

The third reason relates to the recent proliferation of bond funds. This has meant that many investors, hungry for yield, have been attracted into the bond market indirectly through a bond-based unit trust. Yet they may have ended up being disappointed by its performance. This book will attempt to explain why this has happened. And we'll suggest what to look for when picking a fund like this in the future.

A fourth reason is that it is getting easier to deal in bonds. You can deal in UK government bonds through a number of online dealing services. This book will show you how. In addition, many spread betting services also allow you to take a view on the trend in interest rates and bond prices – not just UK government bonds, but also those of other countries.

Finally, many continental European investors have been habitual bond investors. It is one of the distinctive aspects of the British private investor market that so much attention is paid to equities. Sparked by big privatization issues like Deutsche Telekom and the listings of shares on the Neuer Markt and its equivalents, share investing has grown in popularity in Germany and elsewhere on the continent in recent years. But bonds still have a big place in continental investing culture. It is often

It is often said that the archetypal investor in Eurobonds is an affluent Belgian dentist.

said that the archetypal investor in Eurobonds (bonds issued by governments or big companies in currencies other than their own) is an affluent Belgian dentist. True or not, many investors with surplus cash value investments that offer a predictable return without undue risk.

You might find the idea of the British investing culture becoming more like Europe's less than appealing. But bonds have been popular there for just this reason and some others: a reliable return; some tax breaks; the benefits of compounding investment income.

Bonds don't have to be boring

Bond prices move in the opposite direction to yields. If bond prices rise, their yields fall, and vice versa. Bond yields are inextricably linked to interest rates. If rates rise, bond yields usually go in the same direction, producing a fall in price. The opposite is true if rates fall. We'll explain why this happens later, but what it means is that bonds are one way of taking a view on the likelihood of a rise or fall in interest rates.

If you buy bonds, you are in good company. Insurance companies use bonds as a way of guaranteeing that they have the money available to pay policyholders and pensioners years into the future. Bond markets are big. Trade in many bonds, especially those issued by governments, is extremely active.

Table I.1 shows the relative value of the government bond and the equity markets respectively in several different countries. When looking at this table, remember that in the USA and UK the corporate bond market is at least as large as, if not larger than, the government bond market.

Table I.1 Size of bond markets versus equity markets

Market capitalization in bn		Equities	Bonds**
USA	USD	12 300	1881
UK	GBP	1 580	226
Japan	JPY*	372	317
Germany	EUR	754	565
France	EUR	997	528
Italy	EUR	504	574
Euro-zone	EUR	6 645	2497

*trillion   ** government bonds only
Sources: Bloomberg; Morgan Stanley Dean Witter; FTSE International

Last of all, if you own only shares, the bond markets are still important to you. Many companies issue bonds in addition to equity. If you own shares in a company which has also raised capital in the bond market, you need some appreciation of the terms of the bonds to make a proper judgement on the shares.

Some bonds may be convertible in shares in the same company, or may be exchangeable into the shares of another company. You need to know how these mechanisms work and what they mean for your company's earnings per share, cash flow, gearing and other vital numbers. While ostensibly investing in shares may seem to offer more variety, bond markets provide variety in a different way.

A share in a company has common features across many markets: the variety comes in the diversity of companies that issue them. In the case of bonds, issuers are fewer in number. (The government is a single issuer and not all companies float bonds.) But there are dozens of different styles of bond that can be and are issued. Each has its particular features and characteristics. The combination of fewer issuers and a variety of bond types creates a diversity of products in which to invest that is as rich as the equity market.

> Is the prospective return on offer adequate compensation for the risks involved in making the investment?

As in equity markets, bond investors have to satisfy themselves on one key question. Is the prospective return on offer adequate compensation for the risks involved in making the investment? The rest of this book looks in turn at different aspects of investing in bonds. Chapters 1 to 4 cover the following topics:

- What are bonds, how do they differ from shares, and why should you invest in them?
- How to analyze and value bonds, and the tools you need to make decisions about them.
- The external events and market technicalities that drive bond markets.

Chapters 5 to 10 look at each of the main segments of the bond market in turn, including:

- government bonds
- corporate bonds
- Eurobonds
- other types of bond.

The book also looks at the technicalities of dealing in bonds, selecting a broker, where to find information on bonds and, last but not least, the characteristics of collective investment in bonds, their advantages and drawbacks.

This echoes what I think is the main theme of this book. Bonds are for the most part simple to grasp, at least from the standpoint of the way private investors use them. This book is about highlighting the information you need and the judgements you need to make. By the end of the book I hope that you will be as confident in assessing the bond markets and dealing in bonds and bond funds as you are at dealing in shares.

What bonds are and why you need them

Most of us are familiar with the idea of borrowing money. We might borrow from the bank to finance some home improvements, take out a loan to buy a car, or borrow through a mortgage bank to buy a house. Whether it's a home improvement loan, car loan or mortgage, the principle is the same. You pay interest on the debt to the lender and eventually you have to repay the amount you borrowed.

A bond is the same principle on a larger scale. A bond is an IOU that you can buy and sell on the stock market. In this case the 'borrower' might be the government or a company. The holders of the bonds are the lenders. They receive interest payments according to the terms of the bond. Eventually, at the bond's maturity date, the amount owed to each bondholder will be repaid in full.

Bonds versus loans

It doesn't take a genius to see that there are plenty of differences between borrowing money from a bank and issuing a bond to investors. Perhaps the biggest difference is that if you borrow from a bank it is simply a two-way arrangement between you and the bank. If, on the other hand, a company borrows by issuing a bond, all of those buying the bond are each lending a part of the total. This has other implications too. Having bought the bond, one of the holders may decide for his own reasons that he doesn't want it any more. This highlights the second crucial difference between bank loans and bonds.

Borrow from a bank and you have only one institution to deal with. Issue a bond and you need to have a mechanism for dealing with the fact that not all bondholders will want the loan to be outstanding for the same length of time. Some may buy the bond, ostensibly for the long term, but then need to sell for a variety of different reasons.

The difference between a bond and a bank loan is that a bond has fixed terms. These give both the bondholders and the issuer certain rights. The rights inherent in the smallest amount of the bond are identical. Any piece of the bond issue is interchangeable with any other. So this means that, just like shares, bond holdings of any size can be bought and sold in the market. Investors who want to own the bond can buy from those who wish to sell.

> **The difference between a bond and a bank loan is that a bond has fixed terms**

To recap, think of a bond as an IOU from the issuer that can be freely traded, just like a share. Table 1.1 summarizes the differences between a bank loan and a bond.

Bond markets

As is also the case with shares, the 'market' for bonds is not a physical one. It is essentially a network of professional dealers connected by telephones and computer terminals. Share markets went electronic earlier than the bond markets, but increasingly bonds are traded in cyberspace rather than over the telephone.

There are primary and secondary markets for bonds. The primary market covers the process by which new bonds are issued, either by governments, companies, or other organizations. Issues are usually marketed to investors through a network of banks and brokers, often organized in a syndicate, each member of which parcels out their slice of the bond issue to their clients.

In the case of government bonds, for which there is normally a ready market, bonds are simply auctioned off to leading market players. They

Table 1.1 Differences between bonds and loans

	Bond	*Loan*
Borrower (issuer)	Government, company	Company, individual
Lender (holder)	Investor	Bank, financial institution
Interest	Normally fixed	Fixed or floating
Repayment date	Normally fixed	Fixed or open ended
Relationship	One-to-many	One-to-one
Liquidity	Can buy and sell	Not traded
Price	Easily available	Not applicable

are also sometimes sold direct to the general public in much the same way as shares in a privatization issue.

The secondary market represents the way in which the bonds change hands in the months and years following the issue, much as shares change hands on a day-to-day basis. Just as the bond markets are distinct from the share markets, so they also differ from the money market.

The money market is a professionals only market that covers the borrowing and lending of large amounts of money over very short periods, typically from a few hours to six or twelve months. Remember too that bonds which you can trade on the stock market are quite different from savings products that also have the word 'bond' in their title. With profits bonds and guaranteed income bonds are different products with their own particular advantages, drawbacks and charges.

Bond markets are open to professional and private investors alike and cover issues that mature anywhere between 12 months from now to 30 years or longer. There are instances when the money markets and bond markets overlap and instances where bond markets and share markets do too. But they are best thought of as separate.

> Just as the bond markets are distinct from the share markets, so they also differ from the money market.

Bonds versus shares

Even beginner investors are familiar with the idea of shares. At their simplest, shares are best thought of as ownership of a tiny piece of a company, entitling the investor who holds them to a proportionate stake in the assets and profits of the company. One important point about shares, though is that, if the worst comes to the worst, they rank last in line for any pay-out if the company is put into liquidation. If a company goes bust, those to whom the company owes money have first call on any assets. Among those having a prior call on the assets are bank lenders, bondholders and suppliers, who might be owed money for goods and services they have provided. All of these must be paid out in full before the equity shareholders get anything.

In most cases, of course, companies don't go bust. The demands of bondholders, banks and trade creditors are satisfied as a matter of course. and shareholders are entitled to what's left over: steadily growing assets, profits and dividends.

The essential choice you make in owning a bond rather than a share is that a bond has a guaranteed rate of interest and a fixed repayment date: a share

> The essential choice you make in owning a bond rather than a share is that a bond has a guaranteed rate of interest and a fixed repayment date.

has an uncertain return and a price that is always subject to the vagaries of the market. Bond defaults – where the issuer suspends interest payments and even refuses to repay on time – do happen. In fact in the case of corporate bonds, the incidence of defaults has been rising. But there is greater certainty in a bond than in a share, more security and less risk.

This is not to say that bonds are risk free. But if you buy a government bond in the USA or UK, you pretty much know the interest will be paid in full at the specified times and that you will get back the full face value of the bond you bought on the repayment (or redemption) date. This predictability is very useful for investors with certain specific requirements. You may require a regular income, or you may be saving for a particular goal – buying a house, or paying for your daughter's university tuition in ten years' time. Bonds are well suited to providing known amounts at predictable times. Investing in a share portfolio may do this too, but there are no guarantees that it will. Table 1.2 shows the main differences between bonds and shares.

While there are many people who simply choose to have shares in their portfolio and some occasional individuals who just buy bonds, there is no reason why you can't mix the two.

There are many bonds you can buy just as easily through the broker you deal with when you buy and sell shares. Many government bonds can be bought online, although not many investors do this. In a later chapter we'll cover how you go about finding a broker to deal through and whether or not you can deal in bonds through your existing online broker.

Risk versus reward

Limiting your investments just to shares is OK as far as it goes. But bear in mind that professional investors at insurance companies or pension funds

Table 1.2 Differences between bonds and shares

	Bond	Share
Issuer	Government, company	Company
Interest/dividend	Fixed	Variable or none
Security	Priority over assets	None
Volatility in price	Less volatile	More volatile
Risk of total loss	Minimal	Some
Main component of return	Income	Capital
Dependent on	Financial solidity	Profits growth
Outside factors	Interest rates	Market sentiment

who did that would probably be sacked for incompetence. They would be taking too much risk with policyholders' money. Most professionals advocate buying a spectrum of investments, each part of which carries different risks and potential rewards. As market conditions change, they might advocate changing the relative percentage in each different category to get the best mixture of safety on the one hand and potential return (either income or potential capital growth) on the other.

Because it crops up constantly in investing, it is worth digressing for a moment on the nature of risk, and how it fits into the types of investment you hold.

There are various types of risk for any type of investment. In the case of a bond, one obvious type is the risk that the issuer does not honour the obligation to pay interest at specific times and to repay the principal

S I D E B A R

Total return

The trade-off between risk and reward is fundamental to all investment decisions. The reward for investing can come in two main forms, either income or capital growth.

Most investments provide a mixture of the two. This is usually called total return. Total return is the annual yield on the investment plus or minus the percentage gain or loss that occurred in the year. The yield is the percentage the dividend or interest income represents of the amount you paid for the investment.

An *example* makes it easier. Say you paid £1000 for an investment on 1 January. It produced income in the year of £50 and ended the year valued in the market at £1100. The yield on the investment is 5% (50/1000) and the capital gain is 10% (1100 versus 1000). The total return is 15% (5% plus 10%).

Investments vary in the returns they offer. Often shares provide a higher return than bonds, because they go up in value more often than not. In turn bonds yield more than cash, but may rise or fall in price. Higher returns inevitably come with extra risk attached.

The form that risk normally takes in financial markets is the price volatility. The riskier a share or bond, the more its price will swing around. On its own this makes it more risky because the bigger and more frequent the swings, the greater the likelihood that you would take a loss if you needed to sell in a hurry.

amount on the maturity date. This is called default risk or, more generally, credit risk.

For investors who invest, say, in US or UK government bonds, the risk of default is so slight that it can be ignored. UK and US governments have never defaulted on their bonds. Buyers of corporate bonds need to pay much more attention to credit risk. This is because the likelihood of company defaulting is greater than a government failing to honour its obligations.

Of more concern, even with government bonds, is the fact that if you commit yourself to investing in a bond now, you may be forgoing the chance to invest elsewhere on better terms if interest rates rise. Because this concern is so paramount, prices of bonds tend to fall if interest rates rise. If rates fall, however, the higher yielding bond you have invested in becomes more valuable to other investors. Assessing this interest rate risk is an important part of bond investing.

> Assessing interest rate risk is an important part of bond investing.

Another aspect is the risk that while you may have a good return from your chosen bond, when it matures you may not be able to reinvest the money on such favourable terms. This is called reinvestment risk. It is another reason why long-term bond prices rise when interest rates fall. A decent yield available over a long period means that the reinvestment problem need not be confronted for some time.

The various risks that you run when investing in a bond, however modest, are bound up with whether or not and by how much the price swings around. This is called its 'volatility'. Volatility matters unless you intend simply to hold the bond until it matures.

Sharpe Ratio

The ratio calculated in the sidebar on page 13 is called the Sharpe Ratio, named after the American academic who devised it. It is widely used by professionals to compare different classes of investment. When used by professionals it is calculated very precisely, but there are quick ways that ordinary investors can work it out, without going through reams of complex figures and statistical analysis. We'll cover this in Chapter 2 on bond basics.

Bonds in your portfolio

In the end, only you can decide how much risk you are prepared to shoulder in your search for investment returns. In the previous section we raised the idea of a spectrum of investments, each with different likely returns and different risks attached. Your ideal collection of investments (your 'portfolio') could include risk-free cash, highly risky smaller companies and some more stable, high-yielding bond investments.

For the reasons explained earlier, bonds are not entirely free of risk, but you can use them to provide greater solidity to your investments, or you can use them to improve the overall level of investment income you are earning from your portfolio. In fact, the idea of combining a relatively safe investment with high-risk ones that react differently to market conditions is gaining quite a following.

S I D E B A R

Risk and volatility

Risk equates to volatility, but how does it work in practice?

This *example* might help. Over a short time period, Share A's price averages 100p, but it varies from 80p to 120p – 20% either side of the average. Over time the share could show you an annual total return of 15%.

Now take Bond B. Its price also averages 100, but it only varies from 95 to 105. In other words it has just 5% volatility. Its annual return is 8%.

The question is: would you rather have the shares that show a return of 15% but are very volatile, or the more stable bond with a return of 8% and volatility of 5%?

In simple terms, this is the common dilemma that confronts all investors. Incidentally, one way of answering the question posed above is as follows:

Step one: Work out how much you might expect to earn on your money if you locked it away for a year in the bank and didn't take any risks with it. Let's say this 'risk-free' interest rate is 3%.

Step two: Subtract this risk-free rate from the returns on each investment. In the case of Share A, the excess return earned over the risk-free rate is 12%. In the case of Bond B it is 5%.

Step three: Divide the 'excess return' by the volatility. The result for Share A is 0.6 (12/20). For Bond B the result is 1.0.

This means that the bond actually produces a greater return than the share for a given amount of risk.

The way many professionals do this is by investing part of their money passively (in a way that tracks a market benchmark like the FTSE100 index) and part in investment categories like venture capital or hedge funds, which offer returns that are only loosely connected to the benchmark.

Investing part of your money in bonds and part in carefully selected small companies is not quite the same, but it's a variant of this 'core and satellite' approach. The trouble is that it's not really quite as simple as this for many individuals. The amount of money you earmark for share or bond investing may be only a small portion of their total assets. If you need convincing, measure your investment portfolio alongside the equity in your house, the fact that you may have PEPs and ISAs, or an accumulated investment in a personal or company pension.

An Englishman's home, however humble, is said to be his castle. The result is that most Brits have become accustomed to buying property using borrowed money. They have not been put off by instances of 'negative equity', where the value of the property drops below the amount of money borrowed to buy it. The phenomenon of negative equity, though now a relatively distant memory, is a reminder that buying a house with a mortgage is not a risk-free decision. Most people buy on the assumption that house prices will rise. It is often the norm for older homeowners to cash in part of the value of their house 'investment' to provide funds for retirement.

The point is that, though you may not think of it as such, your home is as much an investment as any other asset you own and investing in property with borrowed money is an investment decision with its own risks attached (Table 1.3).

The point is to show that your overall net worth – the value of all your assets minus any borrowings attaching to them – may be more volatile than you think. Adding in some bond investments may not only be a good idea from a long-term viewpoint, but also make strategic sense.

Table 1.3 Differences between bonds and cash

	Bond	Cash
Repayment	Fixed at maturity	Pound for pound
Income	Fixed	Varies
Repayment	Fixed at maturity	Fixed at any time
Early repayment	Market price	May suffer penalty
Notice period	A few days	On demand, 90 days, 1 year

Certainly it argues for considering bond investments more seriously than many investors do. Only in the case of those fortunate investors who have too much income do bonds not make sense!

Bonds and financial market cycles

How and when bonds perform well is a matter of intensive study in the markets. At least two rival investment banks produce annual studies to show the different ways in which bonds and equities have performed in different market conditions over a long period. We'll explore this topic in greater detail in Chapter 3, but the general rule is that bonds tend to perform well when:

- inflation is low
- interest rates are expected to fall
- company profits are under pressure.

These are three constant themes relating to the bond markets. First and most basic is *inflation*. Because the income from most bonds is fixed, inflation erodes their value. As an investor you do not want to hold an asset that is returning an income of 5% of the value of your capital at a time when inflation is 10%. In real terms, in this situation, the value of your capital is being depleted year by year. Hence bonds have few buyers and many sellers when inflation starts to climb.

> Only in the case of those fortunate investors who have too much income do bonds not make sense!

The second theme is *interest rates*. Markets have always been cyclical. In recent years the tendency has been for governments to use interest rates to regulate economic activity. This is not always successful, partly because the response of consumers and companies to movements in interest rates is not instantaneous. At some point in the cycle, interest rates will reach a peak – as they did in the USA during 2000. At that point, and as economic activity slows, there will be an increasing realization that they will be soon be cut. Falling general interest rates means the fixed, longer term returns offered by bonds look increasingly attractive to investors. This increasing attractiveness tends to mean their prices rise to bring about a fall in their yields in sympathy with the actual reduction in rates. Often it happens much sooner than that. Investors anticipate rate reductions and move into bonds well before the rate cuts begin.

The third theme is *corporate profits under pressure*. Other things being equal, share prices rise to reflect underlying profits growth. However attractive the returns from bonds may look because of falling interest rates and low inflation, if corporate profits are continuing to rise, shares will probably represent a more attractive alternative.

The most attractive scenario for bond investors – or at least those who invest in government bonds, which have a low risk of default – is a deflationary scenario of negative inflation. Deflation produces extreme pressure on corporate profits and very low interest rates in an era when prices are actually falling. In this scenario, the fixed income return from bonds stands out like a beacon, not just preserving, but providing increased real purchasing power for as long as the deflation lasts.

> The most attractive scenario for bond investors is a deflationary scenario of negative inflation.

To those brought up in the era of near hyper-inflation in parts of post-war history, such a scenario may seem improbable, but looking back further, periods of price deflation have not been that unusual. Periods when bonds have performed well in the past, though lucrative when they happen, have been the exception rather than the rule. Whether or not that continues to hold true in the future depends on how you view the economic outlook.

> What sort of returns can investors expect from bonds?

But the performance of bonds is not as bad as is often claimed. If we are facing a period of more stable prices and lower profits growth, then bonds may become more of a natural alternative to shares than they have been in the past. What sort of returns can investors expect from bonds?

Table 1.4 shows how UK government bonds (universally known as 'gilts') have performed relative to shares and cash over specific periods in the past. The figures are derived from the annual equity-gilt study published by Barclays Capital, which compares returns from different types of investment since early in the twentieth century.

Table 1.4 tracks the 'total return', that is income plus capital growth, over the periods in question after stripping out the effect of inflation. The results are average annual rates for the period in question. This table dispels a few myths. One myth is that bonds are bad investments. Even over the last ten years, when shares have on the whole been buoyant, bonds are not far behind. The table also shows that bonds only have a really bad patch in an inflationary era and that they do particularly well in the aftermath of a stock market bubble, when shares do especially badly.

> Bonds do particularly well in the aftermath of a stock market bubble, when shares do especially badly.

Table 1.4 Annual average 'real' returns from UK government bonds, shares and cash

	Bonds	Shares	Cash
Last 100 years	1.1	5.5	0.9
Last 10 years	9.4	11.8	4.2
1999–2000	6.1	–8.6	3.2
1999–2000 (USA)	16.2	–14.1	2.3
1960–1979	–2.7	1.1	–0.9
1920–1928	13.9	18.0	10.2
1929–1933	17.4	10.5	6.1
1929–1933 (USA)	10.8	–7.9	8.0

Source: Barclays Capital

Taking the last ten years, though the returns from bonds are less than for shares, Table 1.4 doesn't adjust these figures for different levels of price volatility. Shares are correctly held to be riskier than bonds. A glance at most price charts demonstrates that they are on the whole more volatile than bonds.

As a long-term investor, it is perfectly rational for you to prefer the relative stability of an income-based return offered by bonds to the more skittish behaviour of shares, or to use bonds as a part of your investment strategy to bring a little stability.

There are a couple of provisos here. One is that the returns offered by bonds are generally calculated on the assumption that you reinvest the income, as indeed is the case with returns from shares. This is particularly important for bonds where the fixed rate of return (or 'coupon') is relatively high. In this case the 'income' part of the return will outweigh the capital gain part. This makes it vital that income is reinvested to maximize the bond's earning power. It may, however, be unrealistic to expect that you can reinvest on the same terms as your original investment.

The second caveat is that, as I've stressed before, though bond prices are generally more stable than those of shares, investing in bonds is not risk free. Buy at the wrong time – before the market begins to anticipate a rise in interest rates, or before news that inflation is accelerating – and you could be faced with an instant capital loss as the market quickly adjusts to the new environment. Remember too that not all bonds are the same. We'll look in more detail at different types of bonds in later chapters but the next section summarizes how they differ.

> Though bond prices are generally more stable than those of shares, investing in bonds is not risk free.

Different types of bonds

At the start of this book, I made the point that while shares offered one basic structure and a wide variety of different companies, in the bond market things were a bit different. Issuers are fewer in number: governments, international organizations and large companies. On the other hand, there are many permutations on the basic fixed return and fixed repayment characteristics of a bond. We look at all of these different types in detail later in the book, but here's a flavour.

Government bonds

While seemingly homogeneous, even within the government bond sector there are variations. These relate to the size of the fixed income element in the return and the time left to go before repayment. Government bonds can be long dated, short dated, or medium dated, depending on when their maturity date falls. Bonds are available which have no maturity date. These 'undated' securities are sometimes known as 'irredeemable' or 'perpetual' bonds. High coupon and low coupon bonds are another distinction. Each has attractions for different types of investors, often because of a tax angle.

Index-linked bonds

Because inflation has such a corrosive effect on the performance of bonds, governments in the UK, USA and elsewhere have issued bonds linked to the underlying inflation barometer. These have a relatively low fixed rate, but interest is calculated and repayment of principal adjusted for the movement in a benchmark consumer price index.

Zero-coupon bonds

Another variation on the bond theme, zeros pay no interest in cash terms, but are issued at a massively discounted price to the one at which they will eventually be repaid. The return comes from the capital gain over the period in question. Because they are cheaper to buy, bonds like this can be useful for achieving long-term savings goals.

Corporate bonds

Bonds issued by companies are now an important feature of all major bond markets, and usually at least as big as, if not bigger than, the government bond market. The yields on bonds with the same terms (i.e. coupon and maturity date) will vary depending on the perceived quality of the company issuing them. Independent rating agencies attempt to measure companies' credit standings objectively.

Junk bonds

These are corporate bonds from companies with low credit standing – either unknown companies or well-known companies in poor financial condition. Risk of default is higher. Therefore yields are much higher than normal to tempt investors. Investors have to decide whether the yield is tempting enough to offset the greater risk of default.

Eurobonds

These are bonds which are issued in a currency other than that of the issuer, whether a government, international organization or company. The bonds can be issued in multiple numbers of currencies or a single one. Issuers use Eurobonds to obtain cheaper financing than is possible in their home market, or to match revenue in a particular currency with interest payments in that same currency.

Convertible bonds

These are like conventional corporate bonds, but have an extra component. The bond has a fixed repayment date and coupon, but also carries an inbuilt option that the holder can exercise (or not as he chooses) to convert the bond into shares of the underlying company at a specific price and at a particular time.

Exchangeable bonds

These are convertible bonds, but instead of the bond being convertible into shares of the issuing company, the inbuilt option gives the bondholder the right to convert into the shares of another company. This is often used in corporate spin-offs, such as (in the recent past) France Telecom and Orange.

Table 1.5 is a quick reference table which summarizes the key features and purposes of these different types of investment.

Table 1.5 Key features of different bond styles

Type	Key feature	Purpose
Government	No risk of default	General
Short dated	Short time to run	Lock in short-term rate
Long dated	Long time to run	Lock in long-term rate
Undated	No redemption	Lock in rate indefinitely
High coupon	Income return	Good for low-rate taxpayer
Low coupon	Capital return	Good for high-rate taxpayer
Index linked	Indexed return	Inflation-proof investing
Zero coupon	Deep discount	Saving for long-term target
Corporate	Company credit	Higher yield than governments
Junk bond	Company credit	Extra high yield
Eurobond	Bearer, currency	Higher yield, anonymity
Convertible	Option to convert	Bond plus equity kicker
Exchangeable	Option to exchange	Bond plus equity kicker

In addition to all this, of course, there is a range of collective investments in bonds (including unit trusts, mutual funds and open-ended investment companies). These are actively managed and targeted particularly at investors seeking extra income. In the UK, they can be placed in a tax-free ISA. The performance of these funds varies widely, as do the charges they impose. We'll look in more detail at this area in Chapter 10.

I hope this chapter has given you some inkling of how varied the bond market can be. It has shown that, for certain types of investor and at certain times in the stock market and economic cycle, bonds can be a wise investment choice. They can work as stand-alone investments in their own right, or simply as part of a range of different investments you might hold.

The next chapter looks at some of the technicalities that need to be mastered to make sensible decisions about investing in bonds. Though some of underlying mathematics behind them is complicated, understanding the basic ideas is the important thing. A financial calculator can easily handle most of the number crunching.

IN BRIEF

- Bonds are tradable IOUs issued by governments and companies. They can be bought and sold in the market, just like shares.

- Bonds offer a fixed return and fixed repayment date and therefore have predictable long-term returns. But their prices can fluctuate and they are, therefore, not entirely risk-free investments.

- Bondholders have greater security than shareholders. If a company goes bust, its bondholders are among the first in line to receive the proceeds of liquidation, whereas equity shareholders are last.

- Bond prices are generally less volatile than equities. Bonds can therefore used to introduce an element of stability into a portfolio.

- Bond prices rise and fall in cycles, doing best when inflation and interest rates are falling, and worst when they are rising. Rapid inflation is particularly damaging for bonds because their return is fixed in money terms.

- Bonds come in a wide range of types. Most private investors will find that government bond markets accommodate most of their needs. Private investors can also buy corporate bonds easily through specialist unit trusts.

Bond basics

There is no getting away from the fact that mathematics plays some role in working out which bonds to buy and when to buy them, but don't let this put you off. Most investors who buy shares are quite comfortable (or should be!) about the arithmetic involved in calculating price earnings ratios (PEs) and yields. Newspapers and statistical services provide information like this and often calculating it from first principles is not necessary.

> There is no getting away from the fact that mathematics plays some role in working out which bonds to buy and when to buy them, but don't let this put you off.

Bonds are no different to shares in this respect. Newspapers like the *Financial Times* or *Wall Street Journal* publish a range of bond data. Some financial websites do too. We'll cover where to find bond market information in more detail in Chapter 9. Before embarking on using bonds as part of your portfolio, it is important that you understand what the commonly used bond market terms mean. The underlying maths is less important than grasping the concepts themselves.

I'll try and illustrate the processes and calculations that bond investors go through using worked examples. Remember that a financial calculator is probably all you'll ever need. There are simple bond calculators available at some websites. We'll look at where to find these in a later chapter.

Also in this chapter we are going to deal almost exclusively with calculations that apply to mainstream bonds. Often called 'straight' or 'bullet' bonds, these are those with a fixed rate of interest and a single fixed maturity date, without any extra bells and whistles. Most investors only ever buy these straightforward bonds, and we'll cover how the others work, and the calculations you need to make to evaluate them, in later chapters.

> Often called 'straight' or 'bullet' bonds, these are those with a fixed rate of interest and a single fixed maturity date, without any extra bells and whistles.

Basic bond components

The basic components of a straightforward bond are its price, its interest rate (or coupon) and its maturity date (or redemption date). Coupon is the term used to describe a bond's fixed rate of interest; maturity and redemption date are used almost interchangeably.

Precision matters in bond investing. For example, bond prices are quoted to two decimal places and the precise date a bond pays interest and the date it is redeemed are important. The reason precision is important is that a small variation in any of these variables affects the value of one bond relative to another. Which of two otherwise identical bonds you prefer might depend on whether it is redeemed at the beginning or the end of the year in which it matures – however far in the future that may be.

Price versus par value

If you're familiar with dealing in shares, you may think that the price of a bond is pretty much the same. If so, you would be missing some of the subtle, but very important, distinctions that apply to bond prices. Like share prices, with bonds there is also a bid and offer price – the slightly higher 'offer' price being the price at which you buy, and the slightly lower 'bid' price being the one at which you can sell. The differences between bid and offer prices of actively traded government bonds are usually much narrower than those on shares.

However, this isn't the only important feature about a bond's price. One crucial distinction is that in strict terms bond prices are not quoted in pounds or dollars, but as a percentage of the 'par' value of the bond. Unlike shares, whose par value is often much lower than the actual price of the shares, bonds are usually issued at a par value of 100 (or close to it) and over the course of their life the market price of the bond will fluctuate around this value. Being invariably redeemed at par, they return to 100 at the time the bond matures.

What governs whether or not bond prices stand at above or below par, and by how much, is simply the supply and demand for the bond in the market. Buyers who buy bonds below par value (i.e. if the price they pay is less than 100) know they can be secure in the knowledge that they receive the par full value when the bond is redeemed, making a capital profit as a result.

Those who buy a bond at a premium to par value (i.e. if the price they pay is more than 100), know that they will face a capital loss – albeit perhaps a small one – if they hold the bond until it matures. The other important point about nominal or 'par' value is that it is closely tied to the interest rate or 'coupon' paid by the bond.

Coupon and nominal value

The coupon is the stated fixed interest rate paid by the bond. Why is it so called? On the wall of my office I have a framed certificate for a 25-year bond issued in 1933 by the Societé de la Brasserie de Lutece. An integral part of the certificate is 50 separate numbered coupons, each one representing a voucher for half a year's interest. The holder of the bond simply clipped a new coupon each time an interest payment date came around and sent it to the company, which then paid the interest due. The point about the coupon is that it is fixed by reference to the par value of the bond, not the price the holder paid for it. The buyer of the bond may have paid more than the par value or less.

In either case, there is no simple or practical way the issuer can administer the interest payments due to bondholders on the basis of the price that was paid, or the current market price of the bond. It can only do so on the basis of the nominal value of the bonds that the bondholder acquired – that is, the value of the holding if the par value of 100 had been paid (Table 2.1).

The distinction between nominal and par value is a subtle one. Nominal value is expressed in pounds, dollars, Euros or whichever currency the bond is denominated in. Par value is expressed as a figure or a percentage. A good way of understanding nominal value is that it is the amount of money the holder will receive when a bond is redeemed.

> A good way of understanding nominal value is that it is the amount of money the holder will receive when a bond is redeemed.

Table 2.1 Par value, nominal value, price and income: bonds versus shares

	Bonds	Shares
Par value	Face value of bond	Minimum price for issue of new shares
Expressed as	100%	Pence
Price	Close to par (above or below)	Usually well above
How dealt	Bid-offer spread	Bid-offer spread
Income	Fixed coupon	Variable dividend
Accrued income	Yes	No

So £1000 of nominal value of a bond with a coupon of 6% will pay £60 of interest each year. The figure is the same whether the holder of the bond paid 95% of nominal value for it or 105%. It is vital to be clear on this because it influences many other parts of the way bonds are valued.

To recap, the coupon is in effect a fixed percentage of the par value of 100. The amount of gross interest received by the holder is the coupon multiplied by the nominal value of the bonds held, irrespective of the price that was paid for the holding.

There are some other points to make about the coupon. One is that bonds differ in the way in which interest is paid. Bond interest is paid either once a year or six-monthly in equal instalments. Hence a bond with a 6% coupon might pay 3% interest on 6 June and 3% on 6 December each year of its life, the last interest payment of all being on 6 December of the year the bond is redeemed. On that occasion, the holder of the bond will receive the nominal value of the bond plus the final interest payment.

The second point is that although bond yields are almost invariably stated gross, bond interest is sometimes paid net of tax. In the UK, for example, most taxpayers receive interest on government securities after deduction of the tax credit, although low taxpayers or non-taxpayers can receive it gross.

Dirty or clean prices?

When someone buys a bond for the first time, they are sometimes surprised to find that a small extra amount has been added to the price they thought they had paid for the bond. The reason is that an amount is added for 'accrued interest'. The reasoning behind accrued interest is that although a bond issuer might pay the interest due on a bond on two specific dates, the bond earns (or accrues) interest every day between one payment date and the next. Each day that elapses from the last payment date, the holder of the bond earns a little bit of the next interest payment.

> Bondholders rarely sell, and bond buyers rarely buy, precisely on the day interest payments are received.

Bondholders rarely sell, and bond buyers rarely buy, precisely on the day interest payments are received. If someone buys a bond half-way between one interest payment date and the next, they are logically entitled to only half the interest for that period. When the next interest payment falls due, however, it is simply impractical for the bond issuer to work this out, apportioning a different amount of interest to each buyer who bought or holder who sold part way through the period. So the full amount of interest due is simply credited to every holder of the bond on the books at the payment date, irrespective of when they bought it.

The result is that the system of accrued interest has been devised to compensate the seller of a bond for the interest earned between the last payment date and the date the bond was sold. The new holder of the bond will automatically receive the full interest payment, even though he has only earned part of it (Table 2.2).

Instead, the buyer of the bond pays and the seller receives the accrued interest. This ensures everyone's share of the interest payment is a fair reflection of the length of time between payments that they have each held it.

How is it calculated? As shown in the example, the convention is to divide the annual coupon by 365 and then multiply by the number of days that have elapsed from the last interest payment and the day the deal was settled. Hence if a bond with a 6% coupon changed hands 61 days after the last interest payment date, 61/365 or one-sixth of the annual coupon of 6% would be added to the price paid by the buyer.

In this case a buyer quoted a price of 98 receives a contract note quoting a price 98 + 61 days accrued interest, and in round figures actually pays 99 (98 plus 61/365 times 6%). On the other side of deal, the price the seller receives is topped up by the 61 days of accrued interest paid by the buyer.

Table 2.2 How accrued interest works

Bond: Government of Ruritania 6% 2015

Interest payment dates: 1 June and 1 December

Buyer: Mr Rassendyl

Seller: Colonel Sapt

Price: 98.25–98.50 clean

Trade settlement date: 15 August

Nominal value of bonds traded: £5000

Colonel Sapt is the seller of the bonds though Hope & Hentzau, his broker. He receives 98.25 (the bid price) plus 76 days accrued interest. This is 76/365 × 6% or 1.25. Hence he receives a price of 99.5 or, in money terms, £4975 (99.5% of £5000).

On the other side of the trade Mr Rassendyl pays 98.50 (the offer price) plus 76 days accrued interest, or 99.75. His outlay is 99.75% of £5000, or 4987.50.

Hope & Hentzau are an unusual broker: they charge no commission to either party!

Bond prices quoted by dealers or listed in the financial press invariably exclude this accrued interest element and are known as 'clean' prices. The 'dirty' price is the one that includes this accrued interest element. Remember that accrued interest is based solely on the number of days from the last interest payment and the coupon on the bond. Although accrued interest is added to the clean market price to arrive at the price the buyer actually pays, the price of the bond itself has no bearing on the accrued interest calculation.

Calculating a simple yield

Yields are fundamental to bond investing. Yields allow bonds with different coupons, prices and maturity dates to be compared on equal terms. Share investors are familiar with dividend yields. But bond yields differ in a couple of ways.

First of all, you use gross dividends to calculate dividend yields, but companies typically declare dividends on a net of tax basis. This investor has to 'gross up' (add back the tax deducted) to get to the gross dividend and work out the yield from that. There is no need to do this in the case of bonds.

Second, bond coupons (the equivalent of the dividend on a share) are fixed and stated gross. They are a percentage of the par value. The money amount of gross interest received annually by a bond investor is always the coupon multiplied by the nominal amount of the bond held.

The simple yield on a bond (sometimes called the interest yield, coupon yield or running yield) is not the same as the coupon. As we saw earlier, the coupon is a percentage of the par value of 100. But an investor can pay more or less than the par value depending on fluctuations in supply and demand in the bond market.

Here's a simple *example*.   A bond's coupon is 10% and its price is 90. At par (i.e. 100) the bond's yield is 10%. Buy £1000 of the bond at par and the interest will be £100 a year. That is, the yield is the same as the coupon.

At the market price of 90, however, the bond buyer is still entitled to the full money value of the interest payment, even though he paid less than par. He can buy £1000 worth of the bond for £900, but will still receive the fixed interest of £100 per year.

His return (or yield) from the £900 invested is greater than the percentage coupon, because he has bought the bond at a discount to its par value. The simple yield is 10/90, or in percentage terms 11.1%. Yield = Coupon/Price.

Because the coupon is fixed, it follows that yields move in the opposite direction to price. In the example above, if the price went down to 80, £800 would buy the same £100 of income and the yield would be 10/80, or 12.5%. If the price was 110, the buyer would have to pay £1100 for £1000 worth of bonds and the related £100 of income, hence the yield would fall to 10/110, or 9.09%.

Remember these golden rules:

■ Price above par – yield is less than coupon.

■ Price below par – yield is more than coupon.

■ Price rises – yield falls.

■ Price falls – yield rises.

We'll cover in more detail how bond prices and yields react to different outside stimuli in the next chapter, but the most basic relationship is between bond prices and the general level of interest rates (Table 2.3).

Bonds compete for investors' money. Not just with shares, but with other fixed interest investments such as bank and building society deposits. If rates of interest on savings fall, because the central bank (in the UK, the Bank of England; in the USA, the Federal Reserve) has reduced interest rates, bond yields look more attractive than previously. If this happens, other things being equal, investors will move their savings from the bank and building society into the closest available bond. The extra demand that this produces would raise the price of the bond and reduce its yield.

In real life, if the central bank changes the general level of interest rates, or is expected to in the near future, market prices and hence yields quickly adjust, regardless of whether or not investors themselves react. Therefore the subsidiary golden rules are as follows:

■ Interest rates increase (or are expected to) – bond prices fall, and yields rise.

■ Interest rates fall (or are expected to) – bond prices rise, and yields fall.

Table 2.3   Calculating the running yield

Bond: Government of Ruritania 6% 2015
Interest payment dates: 1 June and 1 December
Price: 98.25–98.50 clean (mid-price 98.375)
Running yield to a buyer = 6% / 98.50% = 6.0 / 0.9850 = 6.091%
Running yield on mid-price = 6% / 98.375% = 6.0 / 0.98375 = 6.099%

The yields commonly used as the yardsticks for bond investing are not quite as simple as this. Bonds are normally assessed on the basis of the so-called redemption yield. This is the return an investor receives if the bond is bought and held to maturity. Before we look at redemption yields, we need to make a short detour to look at compounding and discounting.

Compounding and discounting

Compound interest is one of the wonders of the world. Investors often overlook its importance, even though they may have investments that work on that principle. If, for example, you hold a high-income unit trust, you may have taken up the option to have dividend income reinvested in the fund. If so, you know that each time a dividend is paid, a small number of extra units is added to the holding, which in turn then begins to earn income.

The real power of compounding is rarely fully appreciated. Modest annual returns of 7%, when compounded, will double your capital in ten years. A more generous 10% will accomplish the same feat in seven years. Try it for yourself with a calculator.

> Benefiting from compounding means having the discipline not to spend investment income but to reinvest it. This is cold comfort to many an investor.

Benefiting from compounding means having the discipline not to spend investment income but to reinvest it. This is cold comfort to many an investor. Some bond investors rely on income from their investments to live or to bolster a meagre pension. But the fact remains that compounding is an option for investors, whether or not they take advantage of it. Assessing the relative merits of bond investments has to take this into account.

Let's look at an *example*. You buy (at par) £10,000 of a bond with a 10% coupon and 10 years to go to maturity. The interest is paid once a year at the end of the year. You are able to reinvest the interest at 10%. You can spend the interest you receive, over the life of the bond – 10 lots of £1000 plus your money back when the bond is redeemed, but reinvesting the interest produces a markedly different result. Table 2.4 shows the dramatic effect of reinvesting the interest you receive each year.

In other words, reinvesting each coupon you receive at the same rate produces a return over the life of the bond almost 50% greater than if you had simply spent the money as you received it. This calculation ignores the fact that you may have to pay tax on the interest. It also assumes

Table 2.4 Effect of compounding interest

End of year	Coupon	Interest-on-interest	Cumulative interest
1	1 000	0	1 000
2	1 000	100	2 100
3	1 000	210	3 310
4	1 000	321	4 631
5	1 000	432	6 063
6	1 000	543	7 606
7	1 000	654	9 260
8	1 000	765	11 025
9	1 000	876	12 901
10	1 000	987	14 888
Total	10 000	4888	

that you are able to reinvest on the same terms each time a coupon is received, which may rarely be possible.

For the purposes of comparing bonds, however, this theoretical result is valuable because it is an effective way of incorporating into the calculation of the yield both the size of the coupon and the length of time to go until the bond is repaid. The higher the coupon and the greater the length of time to maturity, the more important will be the interest-on-interest element in calculating the return earned over the life of the bond.

Another way of looking at a bond turns this idea on its head. Instead of compounding the interest let's assume you want to spend the income. You can look at a bond in terms of a series of interest payments, each element of which is further out into the future than the last.

Most people would rather have cash now than cash in a year's time. This is not just because of the 'bird in the hand' principle, but because waiting for money is inconvenient and limits your choices. If you have £100 now, you can either spend it, or invest it to earn interest. If you are to receive the £100 in a year's time, those choices are not open to you. In a real and calculable sense, the value now of £100 in a year's time is actually less than £100, less still in two years' time, and even less than that in three years' time.

This principle, known as the 'time value of money', is the basis for many different types of investment calculation, which come under the broad heading of 'discounting'. The idea of valuing shares on the basis of discounting their predicted future annual cash flows is one example of this.

To perform any discounting calculation, we need to choose a discount rate that reflects the time value of money. This is subjective to a degree, but often by convention a rate is chosen that reflects a short-term, risk-free rate of return. At the time of writing, for example, we might choose the UK base lending rate of 5.5%.

Table 2.5 shows the effect of discounting on the stream of cash (i.e. coupon payments) generated by our £10,000 10% 10-year bond using a discount rate of 5.5%. A financial calculator or set of compound interest tables can be used to work out the numbers.

There are two important lessons to draw from Table 2.5. One is that although the total cash amount of interest paid over the life of the bond is £10,000, the total present value of this series of interest payments is actually only 75% of this figure. Because investors would rather have money sooner than later, more than half of this total has been earned by the end of year five. In terms of present value, by the time this halfway point in time is reached, 56.6% of the total interest has been paid – if looked at in terms of its accumulated present value to the investor. This concept of discounting future interest payments is important in calcuating the so-called 'duration' of the bond, a concept we'll look at later.

Table 2.5 Effect of discounting interest

End of year	Coupon	Present value (disc. @ 5.5% pa)	Cumulative interest
1	1000	948	948
2	1000	898	1846
3	1000	852	2698
4	1000	807	3505
5	1000	765	4270
6	1000	725	4995
7	1000	687	5682
8	1000	652	6334
9	1000	618	6952
10	1000	585	7537

Redemption yields

Keeping in mind the idea of compounding, reinvesting interest payments and earning interest-on-interest, let's now look at the most fundamental of the concepts used to assess bond investments – the redemption yield, or yield to maturity. The redemption yield has three components. We have covered two of them earlier in the chapter. These are:

- the 'running' (or interest) yield on the bond – coupon divided by price
- the interest-on-interest earned if interest payments were reinvested
- the annualized rate of capital gain or loss from the buying price to par.

Let's go a little further into the last point. When you buy a bond, as we discovered earlier, the price you pay will be either above or below its par value. The bond will, however, always be repaid at par. So a bond bought below par and held to maturity will automatically generate a capital gain. Similarly a bond with a market price above par will, if held to maturity, show an automatic capital loss if held to maturity. This gain or loss element is factored into the redemption yield, the annualized capital gain (or loss) being added to (or subtracted from) the other two elements.

Because the calculation is complex, you can calculate redemption yields either from specialized books of tables, reading across from the appropriate maturity and coupon for a given price. Financial calculators now have the facility to calculate redemption yields. The normal form is to enter maturity date, settlement date of the purchase, coupon and price, and then compute the yield. There are a number of online redemption yield calculators, one of which is shown in the screenshot (Figure 2.1). These work in much the same way.

Figure 2.1 Calculatorweb

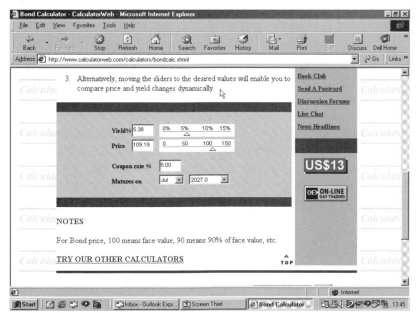

Redemption yields are always counted gross – that is, before any withholding tax on interest or capital. Rather than calculate them, you can often simply look them up in a financial newspaper like the *Financial Times* or *Wall Street Journal*. Nonetheless, it is important to be aware of the nature of the components that go to make up the yield. In some markets income and capital may be taxed at different rates. So even if they have the same gross redemption yield, an investor may prefer one type of bond to another for tax reasons.

> The importance of redemption yields is that they allow different types of bond to be compared and the relationships between them explored.

The importance of redemption yields is that they allow different types of bond to be compared and the relationships between them explored. Bonds with different coupons but the same maturity date can be compared, as can bonds with similar coupons and different maturity dates. All are reduced to the same common basis of calculation and any irrelevant distortions factored out of the calculation.

Yield curves and spreads

Logically, because of the 'time value of money' phenomenon described earlier, bonds that have longer to run to maturity should have higher yields. There are several risks you run by investing in a long-term bond rather than a shorter term one. Not the least of these is that inflation might rise in the meantime and deplete the real value of your investment.

You can sell the bond if this happens, but you might have to take a lower price than you paid. In general terms bonds with longer to go to maturity show greater volatility in their prices and yields than do shorter term ones. Volatility means risk, and greater risk should be rewarded with a higher return – that is, a bigger yield.

So, in normal circumstances, for all these reasons, bonds with longer maturities should have higher redemption yields than those with a shorter time to run. In an ideal world the increments in yield would be steadily greater as maturity lengthened. A two-year bond should yield more than a one-year one; a five-year bond more than a two-year, a ten-year more than a five-year, and so on. Plotting redemption yield against the length of time to maturity for a range of bonds from the same issuer (say, the British government or the US Treasury) produces what is known as a yield curve. A normal yield curve is shown in Figure 2.2.

It is rare for the yield curve to assume exactly the form shown in Figure 2.2. Often there may be kinks in it. It may turn up abruptly at the very

Figure 2.2 Normal yield curve

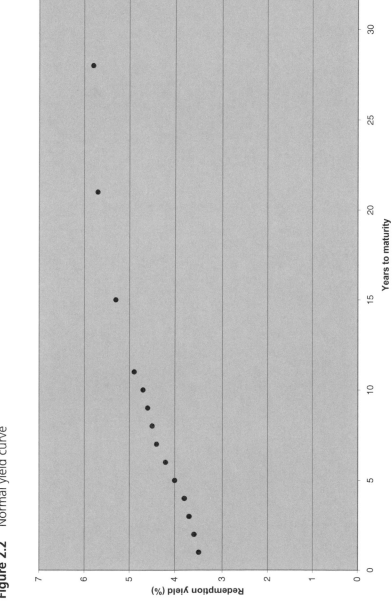

Figure 2.3 Inverted yield curve

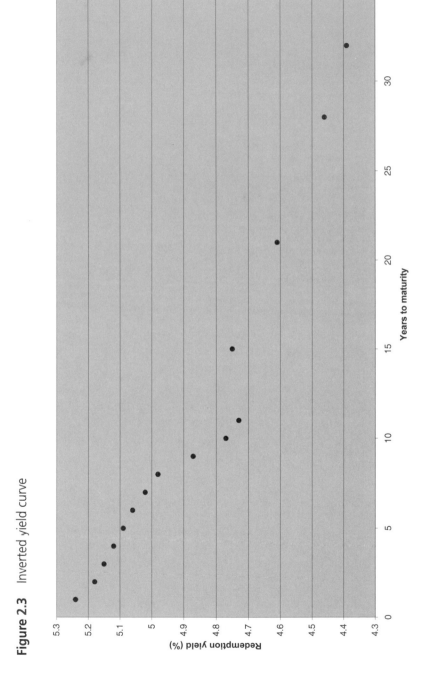

short-term end, or the whole curve may be inverted, that is to say, instead of sloping up from left to right, it will slope the other way. In early 2001, the yield curve in UK government securities (gilts) looked as shown in Figure 2.3.

The phenomenon shown in Figure 2.3 is unusual because it means that short-term yields are higher than long-term ones; the reverse of what the 'time value of money' would lead you to think is normal. The explanation is often that external factors are producing the distortion. We will examine these in more detail in the next chapter. Suffice to say that it means that short-term interest rates are artificially high and may be due for a fall, or that some other factor is driving the price of long-term bonds ever higher, and depressing their yields to unduly low levels.

Because of the standardized way in which they are calculated, and because certain bonds have an infinitesimally low risk of default, differences between redemption yields on bonds with otherwise similar features can be revealing. US Treasuries are, by convention, the benchmark against which all other bonds are measured. The difference between yields of bonds of the same maturity is known as the 'spread' (or occasionally 'basis') and is usually measured in basis points. Basis points are a way of converting small differences in yield to a more normal number. One basis point (bp) represents one-hundredth of 1%: hence a bond yielding 7% when the comparable US Treasury bond yielded 5% would have a spread of 200 bp.

Spreads allow investors to see a pecking order of bonds, as determined by the market. If the US 10-year bond has a yield to maturity of 5%, the 10-year bond issued by Ruritania has a yield to maturity of 6%, and Transylvania's 10-year bond a yield of 6.5%, Ruritania's spread of 100 bp is smaller than Transylvania's 150 bp. Both are judged by the market to be of lower quality than the US bond, but of the two, investors see Ruritania's as the slightly better risk (Table 2.6).

A bond's standing in the sort of pecking order shown in Table 2.6 depends on several factors – the perceived risk of default, the currency in which the bond is denominated and the prospects for it (prospects of a

Table 2.6 How spreads are used to establish the 'pecking order'

Bond issue	Coupon	Maturity	YTM	Spread vs US Treasuries (bp)
Ruritania	5.0	2012	6.00	100
Transylvania	5.5	2012	6.50	150
Zog	7.0	2012	6.86	186

strong currency might increase a bond's attractiveness and therefore reduce its spread), and the likely rate of inflation in the country concerned – which is the other side of the same coin.

Expected higher rates of inflation – perhaps presaged by looser money policy – will erode the value of the bond's interest payments. If this looks likely, investors will demand higher bond yields to compensate. Spreads are crucial when assessing international bonds and bonds issued by companies. If you compare the differences in spreads on bonds of the same maturity issued in the same currency, the difference will mainly reflect perceived differences in credit quality – that is, the likelihood or otherwise of default.

Duration

The final key basic measure to be used when assessing a bond is its 'duration', which embodies all of the concepts referred to earlier. Duration is not a synonym for maturity. Rather, it is a way of assessing the essential difference between two bonds that have similar maturity dates and yields.

> If you compare the differences in spreads on bonds of the same maturity issued in the same currency, the difference will mainly reflect perceived differences in credit quality.

Duration takes as its starting point the fact that bonds are essentially made up of a series of cash payments, each of which has a present value (see the section on discounting earlier in this chapter). In all bonds there are: coupon payments; interest on interest; capital gains or losses on redemption and repayment of principal at the end of the bond's life (Table 2.7).

The duration of the bond in Table 2.7 is about 8.5 years. This is the point at which 50% of the present value of total cumulative interest and principal has been received. In other words, adjusted for the time value of money, the average life of the bond is 8.5 years. After 8.5 years have elapsed, the original investor in the bond at the time of its issue will have received, in real terms, half his interest and money back, and receive the remaining half between then and the maturity date some 18 months later.

In a bond with a low coupon, more of the return comes from the gain in price that accompanies the run-up to redemption: less cash flow accrues in the earlier years of the bond's life. The reverse is true in a bond with a high coupon. The duration is in effect the weighted average life of the bond, taking into account the timing and size of all the cash flows

Table 2.7 Calculation of duration on £10,000 nominal 10% 10-year bond (annual coupon)

Yr	Principal (P) or interest (I)	Payment	Present value (disc. @ 5.5% pa)	Cumulative interest and principal
1	I	1 000	948	948
2	I	1 000	898	1 846
3	I	1 000	852	2 698
4	I	1 000	807	3 505
5	I	1 000	765	4 270
6	I	1 000	725	4 995
7	I	1 000	687	5 682
8	I	1 000	652	6 334
9	I	1 000	618	6 952
10	P+I	11 000	6435	13 387

that make up its return. At some point during its life, the present value of remaining interest payments and return of principal will exactly match the interest payments that have already occurred and which, because they have occurred closer to the present day, will have been discounted more leniently.

For bonds that have a coupon, however low, duration is always shorter than the time to maturity. The higher the coupon, the shorter the duration and, in general terms, the less volatile the bond's price. The reason is that the higher coupon means interest-on-interest is a higher proportion of the overall return on the bonds and exerts a stabilizing influence. Zero-coupon bonds are the most volatile of all. Their duration exactly equals their time to maturity, since all of the return comes with the return of principal when their time is up.

You can use spreadsheets and online calculators to calculate duration. It is also worth noting that duration can be calculated just as easily for a group of bonds as for a single one.

IN BRIEF

■ Bond investing entails grasping some relatively simple mathematical concepts. Financial calculators and spreadsheets can do most of the hard work.

■ Bonds are issued and repaid at their par value. Interest is calculated as a percentage of this par value, not the price paid for the bond.

■ Bond interest is earned daily. When you buy a bond, the interest accrued since the last interest payment date is added to the price. Bond prices are 'clean' (i.e. exclude accrued interest).

■ The running yield on a bond is the coupon divided by the price.

■ The redemption yield is the annual total return an investor will receive if the bond is held to maturity and all income received is reinvested. It also includes any capital gain (loss) that will accrue if the bond is bought at a price below (above) par.

■ Duration is the weighted average life of the bond, as measured by discounting the expected flow of interest payments and principal repayment from the bond. The longer a bond's duration, the more volatile will be its price.

■ Bonds are compared on the basis of their redemption yields and often measured against a risk-free benchmark (typically a government bond of similar maturity). The difference in yield (or spread) between the two measures the issuer's perceived soundness.

■ Yield curves plot the redemption yields of bonds of different maturities from the same issuer (typically government bonds). A normal yield curve slopes upward – the longer the maturity the higher the yield.

■ Many bond variables (redemption yields, spreads, and so on) are published in financial newspapers and websites.

chapter three

What drives bond markets

If you've bought and sold shares, the chances are that you're aware of a variety of influences that can make prices go up and down. It could be changes in an analyst's predictions, comments from the company's management team, or movements in the market as a whole.

The same is true of bonds. There are ways of valuing bonds that are different from the tools you use to assess shares, just as there are influences on bond prices that are different from the influences over share prices. Getting a feel for how these different factors will affect the way bond prices move is no different from the expertise you may develop for understanding share prices.

Like shares, bond prices can move in unexpected ways. External events affect bond prices just as much as shares. They catch out even the most experienced players in the market. Examples of this have included the Kobe earthquake in Japan and the

> Like shares, bond prices can move in unexpected ways.

decision of the Russian government to default on some of its bonds in August 1998. Both sent tremors through both stock and bond markets. The rest of this chapter explains the main influences over the bond markets and why they work as they do. I've illustrated the narrative with some stories and examples to bring some extra colour.

Economic pronouncements

The balance of supply and demand in the market is what drives bond prices. Movements in bond prices are mirrored in their yields. But the factors that motivate buyers and sellers are what really matter. Interest rates and inflation are the two overriding influences on the bond market. Why should this be so? First, let's deal with interest rates.

> The balance of supply and demand in the market is what drives bond prices. Movements in bond prices are mirrored in their yields.

The examples in previous chapters show that bond prices and yields move in opposite directions. If prices go up, yields fall, and vice versa. Bonds compete with other forms of investment for the money of savers. They compete especially with those that offer a fixed return, such as bank deposits for example. The rates of interest offered by banks on deposits are governed by two factors. One is the length of time savers are prepared to lend for. A one-year fixed deposit will return more than one that can be cashed after 90 days, which in turn will return more than an account that can be drawn on without notice.

The other factor is the bank's own cost of money. This is linked to the interest rates set by the central bank. If the Bank of England reduces interest rates, savers will pretty soon notice that their instant access deposit is earning a lower rate of interest. If a government bond were offering a higher return – as measured by its yield – it would make sense for a saver to switch. If enough people did the same thing, the flow of money into the bond would raise its price and lower its yield by sufficient to match the drop in the general level of interest rates. In reality it doesn't need savers to behave like this. A reduction in interest rates will produce a more or less automatic mark-up in prices by bond market makers and create the appropriate drop in yield.

The whole process works in reverse if rates rise. Interest rates on bank deposits outshine bond yields, and dealers mark down bond prices until yields rise by sufficient to match the rate increase. If this sounds fairly

S I D E B A R

The Fed's mangled language

Taken together, and with inflation contained, these circumstances have called for a rapid and forceful response of monetary policy. The longer term advances in technology and accompanying gains in productivity, however, exhibit few signs of abating and these gains, along with lower interest rates, should support growth of the economy over time.

Nonetheless the Committee continues to believe that against the background of its long run goals of price stability and sustainable economic growth and of the information currently available, the risks are weighted mainly towards conditions that may generate economic weakness in the foreseeable future. (Federal Reserve release, January 2001) simple, it's worth pointing out that in practice it doesn't quite work like this. This is because investors often try and anticipate things by buying bonds ahead of an expected rate cut, or by selling if they expect rates to rise. As we'll see later, other parts of the market often provide a strong steer about where the market expects rates to be in a few months' time.

The importance of movements in interest rates to bond prices is why the pronouncements of the current Federal Reserve Chairman, Alan Greenspan, or in Britain's case, Bank of England Governor Sir Eddy George and the Monetary Policy Committee are watched so closely. In turn, because Alan Greenspan's utterances in particular are so closely watched for hints as to the future direction of interest rate policy, they are often couched in ambiguous or downright convoluted language (see sidebar on p. 42).

Alan Greenspan may get frustrated by the market's hanging on his every word. The markets have such confidence in him that they rely on his continuing in robust good health, so much so that when a friend asked, 'How are you Alan?' he is reported to have replied lugubriously, 'I'm not allowed to say.'

Because interest rate policy has such a pervasive influence on bond markets, and because the comments of central bank bosses are often deliberately opaque, commentators and bond market investors tend to try and predict what might happen. They do this by focusing on key bits of economic data that might in turn influence central bank thinking on whether or not to make changes in interest rates.

The sheer scale of the punditry that has developed around the interpretation of economic data is a phenomenon in itself. The economists and market strategists at leading brokers and investment banks as well as independent think tanks all make forecasts. It might lead you to the conclusion that there is no real problem interpreting the numbers and that the data are pretty much cut and dried.

> The sheer scale of the punditry that has developed around the interpretation of economic data is a phenomenon in itself.

In the UK, for example, there are around 30 different City-based forecasting organizations, and a further 15 outside the City of London looking at around 25 different main economic variables. Most of these are the subjects of published statistics on a regular monthly basis. The accuracy of the forecasts sometimes leaves a lot to be desired, but the unduly close following of the numbers is more alarming. Investment bank forecasters are essentially paid to interpret the numbers in such a way as to encourage clients and traders to make buying or selling decisions. Not surprisingly, they may often give small percentage changes in a supposedly important piece of economic data an importance that they do not deserve (Table 3.1).

Table 3.1 Economic forecasts and forecasters

What items are forecast?	Who forecasts them?	
	City	Other
GDP		
Private consumption	ABN Amro	BSL
Government spending	Barclays	Cambridge Econometrics
Fixed investment	Barclays Capital	CBI
Change in stocks	Capital Economics	CEBR
Domestic demand	Charterhouse	DRI
Exports and imports	Credit Lyonnais	EIU
RPI	CSFB	Henley Centre
Average earnings	Daiwa	ITEM Club
Interest rates	Deutsche Bank	Liverpool Macro Research
Oil prices	DKW	NIESR
Money supply	Economic Perspectives	OEF
Employment	Goldman Sachs	Primark WEFA
Industrial production	Hermes	EC
Manufacturing output	HSBC	OECD
World trade	JP Morgan Chase	IMF
Current account	Lehman Brothers	HM Treasury
PSNB	Lombard Street	
	Merrill Lynch	
	MSDW	
	RBS	
	SSSB	
	Societé Générale	
	Standard Chartered	
	Warburg Dillon Reed	
	WestLB Panmure	
	Williams de Broe	

Source: HM Treasury

Small variations from the consensus in figures for the monthly inflation rate – the difference between a 0.3% change and a 0.2% change – might be deemed highly significant. In reality they are barely outside the bounds of statistical error. They may be the result of one-off factors and be revised a few months later. Many government statistics are subject to revision at a later date. Needless to say, the impact of revised figures is often somewhat less than the initial announcement.

We started out by observing that interest rates and inflation were two main influences on bonds. The previous paragraphs covered interest rates, but what about inflation? Inflation remains a bond bugbear, even though some observers believe the recent long period of rising prices is over. The corrosive effect of inflation on bonds is a pretty obvious one. Anything that offers a fixed return on the amount invested looks less attractive if inflation increases. If a bond yields 5% on your original purchase price and the inflation rate rises to 6%, it doesn't take rocket science to work out that you will suffer. While the inflation rate remains at that level, the value of the interest you receive and the capital you have invested is being eroded in real terms. At times like this, bond yields will generally rise to compensate new buyers for the effects of inflation. This is no consolation to those who bought at the earlier lower yield basis. Because yields have risen, prices will have fallen – to leave them showing a capital loss for as long as the trend persists.

In inflationary conditions, assets like property tend to offer the safest real return. Shares can do well, but inflation is often their enemy too, since rising costs can outstrip the ability of companies to put up prices to consumers. Even if statistics could be relied upon and the trends in the numbers were clear-cut, predicting their effect on the bond market is not as easy as you might think. Falling interest rates and benign inflation do not necessarily co-exist. Economic policy objectives may have conflicting effects.

Here are two examples. First, to keep inflation low, governments may need to raise interest rates to damp down demand. The bond market will find higher rates an unattractive prospect. Second, for many governments too, interest rate policy is bound up with keeping the foreign exchange value of the currency constant. Overseas investors may find your bond market less attractive if one result of reducing interest rates is to precipitate weakness in the international value of the currency. Nothing is entirely clear-cut.

Fear and greed

The twin emotions of fear and greed drive many parts of the investment scene. The bond market is no exception. The interplay between fear and greed is a reflection of the two-sided nature of all investments: greed for returns on the one hand, and fear of losses on the other.

The twin emotions of fear and greed drive many parts of the investment scene. The bond market is no exception.

Faced with an extremely uncertain environment, most people will opt to place their savings in the safest form possible. Banks are only human and on occasion have been known to fail (the rarity of bank failures is a relatively recent phenomenon and still not entirely unknown). What could be safer, therefore, than an IOU issued by the government? This is the ultimate attraction of a government bond, or at least one from the USA, UK or Germany. For professional investors faced with extreme uncertainty, short-term government bonds are the only practical home for money. The pros are reluctant to hold cash. Why? Because holding cash is a 'no-brainer', whereas holding bonds looks like a considered professional decision – justifying the money management fees they charge their clients. Hence what is often called a 'flight to quality' is one of the most potent stimulants for bond markets.

In the case of the flight to quality triggered by LTCM, eventually everyone

SIDEBAR

'Flight to quality' par excellence

The best recent example of the 'flight to quality' phenomenon occurred in autumn 1998. This was the time of the near-collapse of Long Term Capital Management (LTCM).

LTCM was a secretive investment fund that relied on high levels of borrowing to magnify the small returns it made on intricate dealings in the world's bond markets. The firm often bought the less liquid bonds that other investors preferred not to own, and sold the more popular 'benchmark' bonds for which there was a readier market.

Once it became rumoured that the fund was in trouble, many investors feared that it would mean a forced sale of the less marketable bonds held by LTCM. They fled to the quality and security of the liquid benchmark bonds it didn't hold, driving the prices up dramatically. The flight to quality was exaggerated because it affected equity markets too.

Fears that the problems at LTCM would affect the finances of the large banks which it dealt with, and so cause a seizing up in the financial system, also led to investors dumping shares and bolting to the safety of bonds.

During the crisis, for example, the FTSE100 index fell by 1000 points from 6200 to 5200 and the Dow Jones from 9300 to 7500 at the height of the panic. Benchmark bond prices rocketed.

calmed down and markets returned to normal, thanks in part to the fund being bailed out by a consortium of banks at the behest of the Federal Reserve. But it is probably fair to say that at least some investors learnt the lesson that the safest bonds were the most freely marketable benchmark bonds issued by governments, rather than the less marketable higher yielding ones. We will cover government bonds in more detail in Chapter 5.

Greed is the other side of the coin. In bond markets, its most common manifestation is a search for yield. In its most extreme form it leads investors to ignore the fact that high returns usually come with high risks attached. Searching for extra yield has frequently led professional investors into bonds issued, for example, by emerging market governments. Or they have moved into bonds issued by a variety of corporate issuers. In much the same way as yields on conventional government bonds have fallen, private investors have been attracted to higher yield bond funds.

There is nothing wrong with either strategy as long as investors recognize that greed for yield brings risk along with it. In the case of emerging market bonds, a big risk is the possibility that they pay interest in a soft currency. As the currency weakens, foreign investors find the benefit of the higher yield is lost and capital value is depleted. Bonds like this are also subject to lower levels of liquidity – in other words they may not be easy to sell at the market price if need be. Finally there is the issue of credit quality. Higher yields reflect the possibility, small though it may be, that the issuer may default and be unable to pay interest on time, or repay principal in full when it falls due. It is the market's perception of this risk that is the important factor. And market perceptions are heavily influenced by credit rating agencies and their views on issuers. This is covered in the next section.

Credit ratings

Credit rating agencies wield considerable power in bond markets. Less in the case of mainstream debt issued by G7 governments, but more so in the case of debt issued by governments in emerging markets, and in the market for corporate bonds. Credit rating agencies are self-appointed guardians of credit quality. Their views can have a profound impact on bond prices and yields. They influence the ability of governments and companies to borrow, and the rates of interest they need to offer to attract investors. Broadly speaking, the lower the credit rating, the bigger the yield spread that has to be offered over a benchmark government bond with the same maturity.

There are a number of independent credit rating agencies, but the two main ones are Moody's and Standard & Poors (S&P). The way credit rating agencies go about rating bond issuers is not dissimilar from the way investment analysts assess a company's shares. Paying detailed attention to the industry in which an issuer operates and the company's financial condition, a company is rated on the basis of its ability to continue paying interest for the term of the bond and repaying principal at the end of the term.

Companies where there is some risk of default will tend to have a low credit rating and find it harder to borrow on reasonable terms. In the case of governments, a rating agency will look at the condition of the economy and the soundness or otherwise of the government's economic and financial management.

> **Companies where there is some risk of default will tend to have a low credit rating and find it harder to borrow on reasonable terms.**

Rating agencies also periodically review ratings and may upgrade or downgrade an issuer on the basis of changed information. A higher or lower debt load, deterioration or improvement in industry conditions, changes in financial management and a variety of other factors can contribute to a decision of this sort.

Issuers are typically given letter-based codes to indicate their degree of solidity, with AAA being the best and anything with a letter C being regarded as poor, if not indicating a company already in default or filing for bankruptcy. Rating is graduated in notches. The four highest are AAA, AA, A and BBB for S&P (the Moody's equivalents are Aaa, Aa, A and Baa). Issuers with these rating are regarded as being of 'investment grade'. Ratings below this are viewed as speculative. Bonds issued with non-investment grade ratings or no ratings are sometimes called high-yield bonds or, less flatteringly, 'junk' bonds.

> **Issuers are typically given letter-based codes to indicate their degree of solidity, with AAA being the best and anything with a letter C being regarded as poor.**

If a company's rating is downgraded, it means it will find it more costly to raise finance. In other words, it will have to offer better terms to tempt investors. In the case of a large company the impact of a rating downgrade can run well into six figures (Table 3.2).

Rating agencies are sometimes criticized for using subtle forms of pressure to force companies into having a rating irrespective of whether or not they need one. On occasion one of the agencies will issue a rating on an unsolicited 'public information' basis, the implication being that if

Table 3.2 Typical credit ratings for senior debt

Rating code	Countries (local currency rating)	Banks	Companies
AAA	USA, UK, France, Germany, etc.	Asian Bank, World Bank, FNMA	GE
AA	Italy, Bermuda, Iceland, Chile	Abbey National, Halifax	Wal-mart, Procter & Gamble
A	Hungary, Korea, Malaysia	Royal Bank, Bank of Scotland, HSBC	BT, Capital Shopping, Norsk Hydro
BBB	Morocco, Colombia, India		Yorkshire Electricity, Daily Mail, Lucent
BB	Lebanon, Kazakhstan, Brazil		
B	Romania, Mongolia, Surinam		

Sources: S&P, Moody's, *Financial Times*

the company were to pay for an official rating and provide the necessary information, its position in the pecking order might improve.

Another criticism the agencies face is that their approach is too inflexible and formula driven and that their staff on occasion may be inexperienced. Also criticized, in the case of sovereign debt, is that the relative strength of an economy may be gauged via a process that simply reflects conventional or currently fashionable economic policy viewpoints. At the company level, there have been instances of rating agencies overlooking distinctive facets of a particular industry, which objectively might have a bearing on the rating.

Whatever the merits or otherwise of the way rating agencies behave, they are a potent force in the market. Depending on your point of view they operate as a more or less unregulated monopoly – or they perform a vital public service. The views of rating agencies are less important for those investors likely to confine their investing to G7 government bond markets. Most of these are rated

> Whatever the merits or otherwise of the way rating agencies behave, they are a potent force in the market.

AAA. The main issue for investors stemming from credit ratings is whether or not the price of a bond, and the yield basis on which it stands, is paying too much or too little attention to the credit rating.

The skill of bond fund managers may be summed up as being able to spot bonds that are less risky than they are perceived to be, and to avoid those where the return on offer does not adequately reflect the risk of default.

Influence from other markets

Futures and options and stock loans are two examples of the way in which activities that are peripheral to bond markets can influence the prices of individual bonds, at least for short periods. Bond futures trade in a separate market alongside government bonds. They allow experienced investors to take geared up positions on future movements in bond prices and interest rates. Traders need only put up a small percentage of the underlying value of a futures contract, although top-ups may be called for if the trade goes the wrong way.

There is some variation between different markets in the way bond futures are designed. It is, however, usual for a basket of bonds of a similar maturity to be deemed acceptable for delivery against the future. This happens in most cases because few markets have a single bond in sufficiently plentiful supply to act as the underlying basis for a bond futures contract.

In the Alice in Wonderland way that futures markets work, even the provision that a basket of bonds may be delivered at some point is more theoretical than practical. Physical delivery is rarely made, trades invariably being liquidated before delivery becomes necessary. It is, however, not unknown for a bond's price to move because it has become the 'cheapest to deliver' bond in the contract's basket.

Another factor that occasionally influences the prices of certain bonds is the fact that traders selling a bond short, perhaps as part of a complex hedging strategy, are required to borrow the bond on the temporary basis for settlement purposes. The bond is returned to lender when the trade is 'closed'.

Lenders are typically long-term institutional holders of bonds, such as pension funds. Some are active short-term lenders of bonds, and use it mainly as a way of generating additional portfolio income to offset against other administration costs. Occasionally, if a particular short-selling trade becomes popular in the market, a particular bond may become highly sought after and deemed to be 'special collateral'. If so the bond's price may react temporarily to the fact that it has suddenly acquired a scarcity value. For the most part, such movements are very small, though important for the traders concerned.

Bonds are also used actively in so-called repurchase agreement (repo) trades, through which bonds are pledged as very short-term collateral. These agreements allow traders to finance speculative short-term positions in the market. Shortage of particular types of collateral for use in repos can also influence bond prices.

Curves and convergence

We saw earlier that one way of looking at bond markets is through the medium of the yield curve. This is a visual representation of the way yields vary according to the maturity dates of the bonds in question. Because of the preference of most investors for liquidity, yields on longer dated bonds are typically higher than those on very short-term ones. It's a version of the same phenomenon which means that your instant access account earns a lower rate of interest than one where you have to give 90-day notice.

> The yield curve is a visual representation of the way yields vary according to the maturity dates of the bonds in question.

Because yields in government bond markets reflect supply and demand and investor expectations of what may happen, the theoretical curve that should slope up smoothly from left to right doesn't always materialize. A curve that slopes the opposite way is known as an inverted yield curve. This is where short-term yields are higher than long-term ones. It is far from rare, but seldom offers clear signals to the market.

The current inversion in the UK yield curve, which began in October 1998, may have been caused in part by the demand from pension funds for longer dated gilts in the wake of the imposition of rules governing pension fund investment (see below). Investors often assume that a flattening of the yield curve will normally be accomplished by a sharp fall in short-term interest rates as set by the Bank of England, and hence a reduction in short-dated gilt-edge yields.

Life is rarely that simple. Take the UK as an example. When economic activity is strong but inflation is low, there is little need for the government to reduce short-term rates, particularly if UK rates are on a par with those of Europe. Cutting rates in this scenario, without reductions being matched by cuts by the European Central Bank in Frankfurt, would simply lead to weakness in the pound against the Euro. This would happen because international companies and investors would prefer to deposit their money in Euros where it would earn a better rate and not depreciate in value.

The ability of pundits to forecast market movements on the basis of the yield curve has been disproved by recent events. The conventional wisdom is that once the inversion of the yield curve has happened, share and bond prices will start to improve. Short-term rates will be cut, boosting prices of short-dated gilts. And because rates have been cut, the economy will expand, boosting company profits and share prices. This theory has worked on three out of the five occasions since the early 1980s when an inverted yield curve has been seen. Bond prices rose, but shares rose more, in the period between March 1980 and June 1981, between September 1981 and May 1982, and between February 1985 and May 1987.

In the long period of recession from October 1989 to August 1992, just before Britain was forced from the ERM, returns from equities were meagre and gilts showed double-figure annual returns. The present inversion of the yield curve began in October 1998, and at the time of writing was still in force. Benefits – in the form of superior returns – from a flattening yield curve may occur, but whether they are caused by it or by other external factors is perhaps a moot point.

Convergence has been another feature that has influenced European government bond markets. Several months prior to adoption of the single currency in January 1999, bond yields in various parts of Europe, notably Spain and Italy, diverged considerably from those of Germany and France. With the adoption of a common monetary policy, a single Euro-zone central bank and the beginning of the issuing of debt in Euros rather than individual currencies, there was no logical reason for the size of the disparity.

As it became clear that the adoption of the Euro was going to happen and that bond yields would essentially be based around those in Germany, yield differences narrowed sharply. This produced substantial price gains for holders of Spanish and Italian government bonds as their yields moved to more or less match the lower yields of German government bonds.

Since Euro-zone currencies have been locked together, the small disparities in yields that remain reflect differences in the perceptions of the creditworthiness of individual governments and their ability or willingness to pursue sound economic policies.

Structural factors

Finally, the bond market is prone to being influenced by technical and structural factors that may seem arcane, but which can be quite influential. One dilemma faced by governments is that fiscal rectitude (or parsimony with public spending, depending on your viewpoint) and strong economic growth have produced significant public sector surpluses. This has been particularly true in the USA and UK. It gives governments the option, should they choose to exercise it, of paying off debt.

Yet, unless carefully structured, if governments pay down debt they reduce the size and liquidity of the government bond market. This in turn may impair their ability to borrow at sensible terms if need be at a later date. However much governments may profess to hold to the path of fiscal and monetary stability, the fact remains that events conspire to drive them off course and sometimes produce the need for borrowing sooner than expected. It's a bit like cancelling your overdraft facility when you have money in the bank. If you then hit hard times and need to reinstate it, the bank may be less inclined to look favourably – or may offer you an alternative that costs more.

Nonetheless, governments find it hard to resist the propaganda value of paying down debt. In the USA, for example, at the time of writing the Federal Reserve, having recently phased out the benchmark three-year note (bond), is now proposing to eliminate its one-year equivalent and also the 'long bond', the 30-year benchmark bond. A recent vote on the issue in a key advisory committee split two-thirds/one-third in favour of getting rid of the 30-year issue. The advocates of abolition argued the case on the dubious grounds that it was inconsistent with predictions that the national debt would be completely repaid within ten years. The same argument suggests that long-term government bonds in the USA will soon be a thing of the past.

Governments also need to bear in mind that certain categories of professional investor need a reasonable supply of top quality bonds across a range of maturities to fulfil their legal obligations. There is a particular case of this in the UK that relates to pension funds and their need to make adequate provision to pay the pensions of the next generation of pensioners. Legal provisions enacted in the Pensions Act of 1995 in the wake of the Maxwell debacle meant that pension funds had to meet certain minimum tests for funding pensions and to have assets that produced long-term income to match their liabilities.

Most UK pension funds were forced by these rules to invest a significant portion of their funds in long-term UK government bonds. This has artificially increased prices and depressed yields. It has been one cause of the inversion of the yield curve noted in recent years, alluded to earlier. The shortage of suitable gilt-edge stock for pension fund investment has been exacerbated by the government's determination to generate budget surpluses and, as a result, there being no need to issue new bonds to finance public spending.

In turn the shortage of supply of suitable stock is compounded by demographic factors, in particular the ageing of the post-war baby boom (now well into their fifties). This category of the population is now stepping up saving for retirement and putting away cash into their pension funds, making the problem even more acute.

S I D E B A R

The curious story of War Loan

At around the time I started working on the stock market in 1970, there was consternation at the price of War Loan. Old market hands tutted as the price in the early 1970s – ravaged by the era's high inflation – fell below 40% of par. By 1975 it had hit 20%.

War Loan is a UK government bond that was first issued by Lloyd George's government in 1914 to finance expected wartime spending. It was sold to investors on the basis that it was their patriotic duty to buy it. It is one of the relatively few bond issues that has no maturity date, known as an 'irredeemable'. Thus its price reflects, in a pure form, the two main influences on the bond market – inflation and the general level of interest rates.

In the course of 1998, helped along by the general shortage of long-dated debt, War Loan's price rose from 55 to 77, providing investors lucky enough to buy it with a total return of close to 50%. It is illiquid and expensive to administer, because it is spread among a large number of small holders – the descendants of the original patriotic buyers.

It may be worth the government redeeming it. The possibility is occasionally mooted. In 1932, the government offered redemption or the option of a reduction in coupon from 5% to 3.5%. Most took the latter option, an indication perhaps of the justified suspicion with which the general population views the government's motives when it comes to debt repayment.

Table 3.3 Gilt-edge stock: amounts outstanding (mid-April 2001)

Conventional				Index-linked			
Issue	coupon	Maturity	Amt (£bn)	Issue	coupon	Maturity	Amt (£bn)
Treasury	7	2001	12.75	Treasury	2.5	2003	2.7
Treasury	7	2002	9	Treasury	4.375	2004	1.3
Treasury	6.5	2003	8	Treasury	2	2006	2.5
Treasury	5	2004	7.4	Treasury	2.5	2009	2.6
Treasury	8.5	2005	10.4	Treasury	2.5	2011	3.5
Treasury	7.5	2006	11.7	Treasury	2.5	2013	4.6
Treasury	7.25	2007	11	Treasury	2.5	2016	5
Treasury	9	2008	5.4	Treasury	2.5	2020	4.2
Treasury	5.75	2009	8.8	Treasury	2.5	2024	4.8
Treasury	6.25	2010	4.75	Treasury	4.125	2030	2.6
Conversion	9	2011	5.3				
Treasury	8	2021	16.5				
Treasury	6	2028	11.5				
Treasury	4.25	2032	13.6				

Sources: Financial Times, DMO

Relaxation of the rules to allow UK pension funds to invest in other European government bonds or in higher quality corporate bonds was recently proposed by a government-sanctioned report. But some observers doubted that even this would solve the problem, since the supply of bonds of sufficiently long duration is limited. In addition, pension funding problems and the interplay with demographic influences is at least as acute in most of Europe as it is in the UK. By implication, Euro-zone pension funds may yet see the same short supply of long-term government bonds.

However this situation plays out, the point is that bond investors need to keep themselves up with developments in this area, because of its crucial importance for the trend in yields and therefore prices in longer dated bonds. The entry of Britain into the Euro would at least offer pension funds the ability to invest in a broader range of government bonds without having to take account of any risk that currencies would be devalued. Yields on the longest dated UK government debt are, for example, currently over 75 bp (0.75%) below the equivalent yields for Euro-denominated government bonds in France and Germany.

> Bond investors need to keep themselves up with developments in this area, because of its crucial importance for the trend in yields and therefore prices in longer dated bonds.

IN BRIEF

- Interest rates and inflation are key influences over bond prices. Bond yields move in sympathy with interest rates. Rising inflation is bad for bond prices, and vice versa.

- Economic data also have an impact on the bond market, mainly because they hold the key to whether interest rate changes are likely or not.

- The relative prices of bonds are influenced by perceptions of credit quality. Rating agencies are influential in shaping these perceptions. Investors need to judge whether or not a bond's price is paying too much attention to credit concerns.

- The shape of the yield curve can indicate whether or not bonds are likely to perform well or badly, but interpreting its movements can be difficult.

- Extraneous factors such as politics, currency movements and market technicalities can also influence bond prices.

- Demand from pension funds for long-term bonds, combined with the government surpluses and hence fewer bond issues, are causing an imbalance in supply and demand for long-term bonds, particularly in the UK but potentially across the Euro-zone.

Dealing in bonds

This chapter covers how to go about dealing in bonds. If you are new to the stock market as a whole, read the general section about choosing a broker. If you already have a broker you can omit this initial section. Later sections of this chapter provide more information for those planning to use their existing broker to deal in bonds.

How stockbroking works

Over the years the image of stockbrokers has varied. In the novels of Trollope and Dickens, they are presented as seedy, disreputable characters. On 1920s' Wall Street, their image changed to that of hard-nosed market manipulators. They prey on unsuspecting private investors, roping them into speculative stocks while they – the professionals – sell out. In the 1950s, 1960s and 1970s the public image of stockbrokers changed to City fat cats in bowler hats and pinstripes. In the 1980s and 1990s the image shifted again to the 'greed is good' yuppie with a Porsche, big bonus and unsocial working hours. These are no more than caricatures. Private client stockbrokers are normal, professional people who have continued, through the ups and downs of the market, to do the best for their clients. They have always sought to offer an informed and personal service.

However, there have been changes to the structure of the market in the UK. One newer feature is that many large firms decided that looking after private clients was too costly and labour intensive. They saw the traditional private client business as out of step with modern investment banking. Here the emphasis is dealing profits and lucrative merger and acquisition fees, not transacting small deals for individual investors.

> Private client stockbrokers regard the service they offer to their clients as the very bedrock of what the business should be about.

By contrast, private client stockbrokers, with some justification, regard the service they offer to their clients as the very bedrock of what the business should be about. The result of this divergence of attitudes is that many smaller firms took the view that competing with big firms for the business of institutional investors would be difficult. They decided to specialize in offering services to the private client. In the past decade or so, many private client firms have merged to spread the cost of investment in systems required by the new market order. The new-style electronic market in shares, which was ushered in by the so-called 'Big Bang' of market de-regulation in the UK in 1986, meant there was no pressing need for regional brokers to maintain offices in London in order to have a presence on the market floor. This change aided the process of consolidation among smaller regional firms.

Many regional firms, for instance, are now represented in one of the main regional financial centres together with offices in a number of adjoining provincial towns. They have kept a regional focus and the personal touch, but benefit from being part of a large organization by spreading the cost of processing and settling deals.

In addition, the idea of cheap, no-frills stockbroking was introduced some time ago and caught on quickly. The idea originated in the USA, but in Britain firms like this prospered from the expansion in share ownership engendered by the government's privatization programme. They also gained market share from traditional brokers whose clients had become dissatisfied with high commission levels. The advent of web-based dealing has also led to increased numbers of clients dealing on this 'execution only' basis.

No-frills brokers base themselves in cheap locations. They operate highly sophisticated telephone or internet-based order-taking systems and streamlined settlement. They simplify administration by having clients hold stock in a broker's nominee account or via a CREST individual member-

Table 4.1 Types of broking service

Type	Dealing basis	Typical fee basis
Execution only	You decide, broker deals	Low flat rate
Dealing with advice	Broker has ideas, you decide	Percentage commission
Portfolio advice	Broader advice, you decide	Fee plus commission
Discretionary	Brokers acts within parameters	Percentage fee

ship. They link client dealing automatically to high-interest bank accounts in order to avoid cheque processing. CREST is the electronic system for settling deals in UK shares and bonds.

The big structural changes in the stock markets since the mid-1980s have increased the choice open to individuals looking to select a stockbroker for the first time. Existing clients of a broker also find it easier to move their accounts. The choice of brokers, in short, is wider now than it has ever been in the past. There are a number of different types of service available (see Table 4.1):

- execution only
- dealing with advice
- portfolio advice
- wholly discretionary.

Execution only

Execution only broking is another name for the no-frills service outlined in the previous paragraphs. There are many broking operations that now offer no-frills dealing, either telephone and/or internet based. Many banks and building societies also offer execution only dealing.

A broker like this offers a dealing service with no advice. On occasion some may offer research on a cash basis, provide subscription newsletters and organize seminars for clients. Frequent traders can expect commission rebates. As with banking, internet share trading is usually cheaper than its telephone-based equivalent.

Execution only broking is popular with experienced stock market investors who make their own share selections. The service is cheap for those prepared to back their own judgement without looking for advice. If you are looking for a father-confessor figure, you will get short shrift from an execution only broker. Others likely to use them include those whose stock market investment is confined to privatizations and other new issues.

> Execution only broking is popular with experienced stock market investors who make their own share selections.

They are not habitual investors, but may occasionally need to sell small parcels of shares as cheaply as possible. Most execution only brokers offer the facility to deal in UK government bonds (gilts) and other fixed income securities such as convertibles. The proviso is that the stock concerned has a security code to allow a dealing price to be accessed.

Winterflood Securities, a market maker specializing in dealing in smaller companies, introduced market making in gilt-edge stocks aimed at 'retail' (i.e. private client) brokers some time ago. Winterflood operates a computerized small order dealing facility that can be accessed by online brokers. This has made it easier for online brokers to offer a service that can cater to bond investors as well as share buyers. In partnership with Barclays Capital and HSBC, the firm recently launched Bondscape, an online corporate bond dealing and information service offered through private client stockbrokers.

Dealing with advice

Most stockbrokers, other than those providing solely an execution only facility, offer this service. The broker charges commission at a standard rate that is more expensive than execution only. The difference is that you have a designated contact name at the firm to deal on your behalf. You can contact this individual on the telephone from time to time for advice. The important point here is that the relationship is two-way. The broker will be reluctant to spend too much time discussing ideas if you don't deal from time to time. If you deal frequently, this may result in the broker taking a more active role by initiating ideas. The package may also include the provision of some basic research. While most clients will be seeking advice on equities, a good advisory broker will also to be able to offer advice on bonds and the bond market.

> The broker will be reluctant to spend too much time discussing ideas if you don't deal from time to time.

The service will not, however, include any more comprehensive advice on how other aspects of your financial affairs should be managed. Other services (such as periodic valuations or the preparation of capital gains tax statements) may not be available or may cost extra.

Portfolio advice

> The next level of service is a more comprehensive one.

The next level of service is a more comprehensive one. This entails the broker discussing your investment objectives. This may include whether you are aiming for maximization of income or capital growth, and the degree of risk you are happy to bear. Other aspects of your financial affairs may need to be explored. The service should include providing information relating to the capital gains tax position on your holdings and how to invest for maximum tax efficiency. Assessing whether or not bond investments constitute a sensible part of your investing strategy should form part of the advice you are given.

Charges are usually an annual fee on top of dealing commissions. This reflects the enhanced level of service. This approach clearly involves the broker taking a more active role in the management of your financial affairs.

Wholly discretionary

This means that the broker makes all the decisions on your behalf and tells you about them after the event rather than before. Some investors find this approach rather unnerving, but a good broker operating in this way should be able to offer you better performance from your portfolio than you could have managed on your own.

> The broker makes all the decisions on your behalf.

In this instance, the broker will take a percentage annual fee linked to the value of the portfolio. If the portfolio enjoys good appreciation, the broker's fee will rise – a worthwhile incentive and one which you should feel happy to accept. You should, however, be able to specify in advance that you wish a certain percentage of the portfolio's value to be allocated to investment in bonds, and to specify what types of bonds would be acceptable to you from a risk standpoint. But remember that the broker will have discretion to act, within the parameters you set, without prior reference to you.

Which to choose?

In many instances the type of broking service you have for dealing in ordinary shares will also be suitable for bond investing. This is especially true if you use a telephone-based 'dealing with advice' service. You may, however, find that some online brokers do not offer much of a service in bonds. Some only deal in equities. Table 4.2 shows a selection of those brokers that specifically offer a dealing service in UK government bonds and also offer online dealing.

Some people find a broker through personal recommendation from a friend, accountant, solicitor or financial adviser. Recommendations like this are subjective. If you are a first-time investor, it is important to make the right choice. You need to exercise your own judgement about which broker will be best for you. You could find a stockbroker simply by consulting the telephone directory or Yellow Pages, but this is haphazard and might, in any event, only give a local list. Many brokers now advertise their services. Consulting the *Financial Times* and magazines such as *The*

Table 4.2 Brokers dealing in gilts (and their other services)

Broker name	Web address	Offline discretionary	Offline advisory	Offer dealing in? UK gilts	European	US shs	Options	Crest Ind membship	Use of nominee
Barclays Stockbrokers	www.barclays-stockbrokers.co.uk	Yes	Yes	Yes	Yes	Yes	No	Yes	No
Cave & Co	www.caves.co.uk	Yes	Yes	Yes	Yes	Yes	Yes	No	Yes
Charles Schwab Europe	www.schwab-worldwide.com	No	No	Yes	Yes	Yes	Yes	No	Yes
Comdirect	www.comdirect.co.uk	No	No	Yes	Yes	Yes	No	No	Yes
Goy Harris Cartwright	www.ghcl.co.uk	Yes	Yes	Yes	No	No	No	Yes	No
James Brearley	www.brearley.iii.co.uk	Yes	Yes	Yes	No	No	Yes	No	Yes
Killik	www.killik.co.uk	Yes	Yes	Yes	No	No	No	No	Yes
Redmayne Bentley	www.redmayne.co.uk	Yes	Yes	Yes	No	No	Yes	No	No
Xest	www.xest.com	No	No	Yes	No	No	No	Yes	No

Note: All brokers in the table offer web-based, execution-only sharedealing

Source: www.linksitemoney.com

Investors Chronicle or *Shares* should yield a satisfactory number of names, telephone numbers or web addresses. Few if any of the firms which a list like this throws up specifically indicate that they offer a service for would-be bond investors.

The Association of Private Client Investment Managers (0207 7247 7080, www.apcims.co.uk) would normally be a good starting point. It has a searchable online directory of brokers dealing in various aspects of the market. The search criteria, however, do not include bonds. So, while it is possible to isolate brokers in a particular area, and those offering online dealing, dealing in traded options and the like, identifying bond specialists is impossible. The reason for this is that many brokers simply offer dealing in UK government bonds as a matter of course.

After drawing up a short list of possible brokers, requesting information is the next step. In response to a request for information, most brokers will send a brochure and form that will attempt to determine your overall net worth and chosen investment strategies. It is an advantage for the broker to know these in advance. Filling out a form like this will help to crystallize these parameters and objectives in your mind at the outset.

A number of other documents are likely to come back from the broker in response to your enquiry. One will be a form you complete to establish client records for the broker to work from. This is a legal agreement, a contract that you enter into with the broker by virtue of becoming a client. This is so that the broker can be assured of payment for transactions being undertaken and to ensure that deals go smoothly. Sign this only when you have picked a broker as your final choice.

Regulatory organizations covering the stock and bond markets also require paperwork to be completed. This is designed to protect you by establishing the ground rules at the outset. In contrast to earlier practice, most firms do not require clients to be introduced to them; nor is there any requirement for a face-to-face meeting before the account is opened and dealing begins. Regulatory oversight and the customer agreement form that new clients sign substitute for introductions and an initial meeting.

However, meeting the brokers on their own home ground is a good idea. Make a point of going to the firm's offices and meeting the individuals concerned. It enables you to make a better judgement about the quality of the firm and the character of the people involved. It's a particularly good idea if you have more than one firm to choose from.

Remember that firms differ in the services they provide. They will charge according to the type of

> Meeting the brokers on their own home ground is a good idea. Make a point of going to the firm's offices and meeting the individuals concerned.

service you require. For example, if you opt for execution only, the charges will be different to a dealing with advice service. Be sure to compare firms and their services on a like-for-like basis, including any additional charges that the firm may make. Some execution only firms have a low headline commission rate, for example, but charge hefty administration fees on top.

How to deal

Dealing in bonds is similar to dealing in ordinary shares in some respects, different in others. Market makers quote bond prices in the normal two-way bid and offer basis. Dealing vocabulary is slightly different, however, as described in the sidebar.

You can deal online in UK government bonds in the same way as you deal in shares, using ticker symbol for the bond. For those unfamiliar with ticker symbols, these are short codes – unique to each stock – that avoid entering the name of the stock in full. There are however some important points to remember when dealing in bonds through online brokers. Inputting prices and nominal values can be confusing (is the price of a gilt 105 or £105, for example?). For safety's sake, it is worth double-checking that the amount of money being committed is what you expected it to be. Better still, if the option exists, input the amount of money you wish to invest. Online brokers calculate accrued interest and include it in the contract note in the normal way.

Table 4.3 shows a list of ticker symbols for the main benchmark gilts. The stock exchange does not, for reasons best known to itself, make these symbols widely available. In Chapter 9 we look in more detail at how to go about finding information on bonds and their prices. The codes for other stocks are quoted in the relevant chapters.

For some reason, dealing in UK gilts, not to mention other types of bond, has acquired an unwarranted mystique. This has restricted the extent to which ordinary investors participate in the market. In the USA the situation is vastly different. By contrast, UK investors with dealing accounts with a US broker will find it remarkably easy to deal in a wide range of US bonds. The choices include Treasuries, municipal bonds, corporate bonds and the like.

> For some reason, dealing in UK gilts, not to mention other types of bond, has acquired an unwarranted mystique.

Online brokers such as Charles Schwab or CSFBDirect (formerly DLJDirect) offer sophisticated trading opportunities for private investors, including the ability to search for bonds meeting specific criteria, the opportunity to buy new issues, the ability to participate in Treasury bond auctions and a range of other services. UK investors can normally open dollar accounts with US brokers simply by wiring funds and completing a US W8 tax form declaring that they are non-resident for tax purposes.

Yet even in the USA, there are odd gaps. Despite the established pattern of bond investing in the USA among retail investors, some third-party quote servers such as Yahoo! Finance do not provide quotes for even the most liquid US treasury issues. Information on the smallest and most speculative NASDAQ stock is available, but none on the world's most liquid benchmark bonds!

On the continent brokers like Comdirect, Fimatex and e-Cortal are moving towards offering seamless pan-European dealing in equities and, by the same token, presumably bonds. A good test of the ability of systems like this to support bond dealing is to access the relevant websites and input the relevant ticker symbol to get a quote. A system that supports delivery of quotes also ought to support dealing in the relevant quotes.

Table 4.3   Gilt-edge ticker codes – benchmark stocks

Coupon	Maturity	Code
7.0	7.6.02	TR2
6.5	12.7.03	T6H3
6.75	26.11.04	T6T
8.5	7.12.05	TR05
7.5	7.12.06	TR6
7.25	7.12.07	T07
9.0	13.10.08	T09
5.75	7.12.09	T009
6.25	25.11.10	T6Q
8.0	7.12.15	TY8
8.0	7.6.21	TR21
4.25	7.6.32	TR32
War Loan	None	WAR
2.5% Consols	None	CN2H

S I D E B A.R

Dealing in bonds

When you deal, a broker will expect, and you need to know in advance, the following:

1. Which bond to deal in: state the stock, the coupon and the maturity date. An example of the way to quote a bond to a broker is 'the Treasury 5% of 2004'. (**Tip**: You can shorten this, for example, the 'Treasury fives of oh-four'.)

2. Whether the order is to buy or sell.

3. The nominal amount you wish to buy or sell, or the amount you want to invest: in the bond market the order might be, for example, to 'buy £5000 nominal of the Treasury fives of oh-four', or alternatively 'invest £5000 including fees in the Treasury fives of oh-four'. (**Tip**: If stating the nominal amount you wish to buy, multiply by the percentage price to find the actual amount of cash being committed.)

4. Whether the order is to buy 'at best' or whether a limit is to be set, outside of which the broker should not deal. (**Tip**: Because spreads are narrow on government bonds and their prices are relatively stable, there is usually little need to set a limit.) Commission paid to the broker is calculated the normal way. The broker will also usually send out a contract note giving details of the transaction. The contract note will include the amount of accrued interest involved in the purchase. (**Tip**: It is not normal for the broker to tell you the amount of accrued interest at the time you deal.)

5. The broker needs to know whether two orders are linked. It is not uncommon in the bond market for investors to switch from one stock to another, perhaps from a shorter to a longer maturity. Telephone brokers are normally happy to take orders for switches, or 'schemes' as they are sometimes called, simply selling one stock and reinvesting the net proceeds of the sale in the other with all accrued interest and commission taken into account. (**Tip**: If performing a similar manoeuvre using an online broker, you will need to enter two separate orders.)

Alternative ways of trading

If dealing in the straightforward bond market is too dull, there are ways that experienced investors can spice things up a bit. Most involve higher risk, but also potentially higher returns. Using the bond market as the underlying basis is no different to the more normal use of these techniques for trading shares.

The three main alternative ways of dealing are spread betting through exchange traded funds (ETFs) and, for the highly experienced and risk tolerant, through contracts for difference (CFDs). I have excluded any mention here of bond futures. The received wisdom is that these are too risky for most investors to contemplate using them. Spread betting is an effective alternative. Spread betting on financial markets has been around for some time.

> If dealing in the straightforward bond market is too dull, there are ways that experienced investors can spice things up a bit.

But what exactly is it, how does it work, what are its advantages and disadvantages, and is it right for you?

Financial spread bets typically feature leading indices and the top 350 UK shares, but they are also available for betting on bond markets. Spread betting substitutes 'up bets' and 'down bets' for buying and selling. In a spread trade you are quoted a two-way price and indicate the scale of the commitment you want to make by nominating the deal size in pounds per point of spread.

In the case of a share, for example, you might be quoted a 'price' in Vodafone of 260–70. Taking a down bet at £10 a point means that if the bid price of Vodafone falls to 210, for example, you would make £500, the difference in points between the selling price of 260 and 210 multiplied by £10.

Though superficially similar, there are big differences between ordinary share or trading and spread betting. Here are a few of them:

- Because they arise from bets, gains are tax free. Betting tax (or the new corporate profit tax that has replaced it) is absorbed by the spread. This is the reason that the spreads themselves are wider than those in conventional equity dealing.

- You can easily go short, without the hassle of borrowing stock. Simply place a down bet. This applies to bonds as well as stocks.

- Spread betting is margined. This provides you with both extra potential returns and higher risks. The risks come from acquiring exposure to a share, bond or index movement using borrowed money (the margin loan).

■ Risk can and should be managed. Stop losses are integral to spread betting and are also incorporated in the spread if desired. Losses are theoretically unlimited, so you need a disciplined trading style. This applies equally to spread betting in bonds as it does to the more normal use in equities.

Leading spread-betting firms such as IG Index are anxious that would-be clients make spread betting only a part of their overall trading. It should be complementary to rather than competing with your other share (or bond) buying and selling. Paper trading at the outset is probably a good idea. There are several online sites that have spread-betting simulations (see Chapter 9 on information sources). Be warned too that before a dealing account is opened you will need to demonstrate a certain level of liquidity and be a UK resident.

All the leading spread-betting firms offer spread bets in bonds and interest rate contracts, often based around the relevant future. You can bet on both the spot price and also the nearest futures contract. At Cantor Index, for example, punters can make bets in the German bund, US Treasuries, UK gilts, Japanese government bonds and short-term UK and Euro interest rates. IG offers a similar choice.

Exchange traded funds (ETFs)

A more direct way of playing the bond market without getting too hung up on selecting individual stocks is to use what are known as exchange traded funds (ETFs). These are listed shares that are cheap to trade which mimic the behaviour of an underlying index. ETFs, sometimes called iShares, are available for leading stock market indices and some industry groups. In North America, however, the devisers of these products have begun basing ETFs around bond indices, first in Canada and subsequently in the USA.

> When ETFs are launched in local markets in Europe private investors will have a new way of investing in the bond market.

Observers expect such products to be launched in Europe in due course. iShares can be bought and sold through a stockbroker in the normal way, produce income and have ultra-low dealing costs. When ETFs are launched in local markets in Europe, as some professional investors wish, private investors will have a new way of investing in the bond market.

CFDs on bonds – a gap in the market?

Contracts for difference (CFDs) are a relatively new tool for investors. They are similar to futures, except they operate without a time limit. In theory contracts can be devised for any reasonably liquid underlying security or index. Investors buy and sell on margin and simply receive or pay the difference (profit or loss) when the trade is 'closed'.

Most CFD operators offer equities and foreign exchange. But there is nothing to stop CFDs on bonds. Yet these are not offered as a matter of course. It's a gap in the market. As is also the case with spread bets, there are big differences between ordinary share and bond trading and dealing in CFDs. Here are a few of them:

- Because the trades operate on margin, you gain substantial leverage along with the extra risks that go with it.

- There is no stamp duty on CFDs, but gains and losses fall within the CGT regime.

- Investors can go long or short, opening up the possibility of doing more complex strategies such as 'pairs trading' (e.g. long Vodafone, short Orange) or yield curve arbitrage (dealing in gilts of different maturities).

- Execution is instantaneous. Guaranteed stop losses are available and, if required, the cost is built into the charges for the margin loan.

- There is a wide range of instruments available, including the top 350 UK shares, main indices and constituents of major European and US indices. In the past bonds have not featured overtly on the list, but there is no theoretical obstacle to them being used.

In the past, many firms have also tried to confine offering CFDs to highly experienced investors and high net worth individuals. This is changing, however. Some firms offer a minimum account size of only £5000 (versus the £25,000 or more asked for by other firms).

All firms, however, want to see evidence that you are an experienced investor before letting you deal.

Bond portfolio strategy

If you have read this far you will appreciate that bonds are far from being the uniform boring investment that many investors imagine. There are circumstances when bonds can offer better returns than shares and other forms of investment. There are more investment choices in the bond market than are generally imagined and there are ways, through spread betting, in which investors can take a speculative view.

S I D E B A R

Bond charting and price analysis – another gap in the market?

Many share investors use charts. But if you look for similar systems for the bond market, you are liable to be disappointed.

There are systems available that apply technical analysis (i.e. analysis of bond price movements over time) to the timing of trades in the bond market. Unfortunately at present these are only available for the US market, even though the principles they use are probably universally applicable.

A good example is the Ultra Market Adviser, devised by Texas-based Ultra Financial Systems. This product incorporates trade-timing systems for both stock markets and for bonds and gold. Using established technical indicators the system generates signals for moving in and out of stock market and bond funds respectively.

Figure 4.1 Ultra

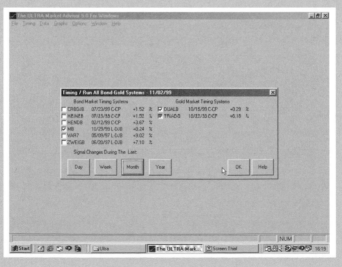

The indicators for bonds typically use comparisons of movements in bond index and individual bond moving averages, the absolute level of and percentage movements in short-term rates and on occasion also indicators such as the inflation rate, to generate their signals.

It is disappointing, and not the fault of the system developer, that no one has yet devised such a product for use by retail investors that looks at analogous data for UK and European bond markets, even though the necessary data are seemingly easily available.

Enterprising investment software developers, please note.

Working out a coherent strategy for investing in bonds depends essentially – as with any form of investment – on knowing yourself and your own particular requirements. Strategies appropriate for a 70 year old with capital but no income may be different from the 30 year old saving for a child's university education. If generalizing is difficult, there are some basic questions that are important.

Is the investment short or long term?

Short-term bond investment focuses around anticipating movements in interest rates. The most effective (but riskiest) way of capturing this may be via spread trading in short-term interest rates futures, but remember that market expectations of the impact of rate changes may be anticipated by the market well in advance.

Is income more important than capital preservation?

If so, buying certain high coupon stocks that stand above par will yield superior income until maturity, although the underlying value of the holding will be reduced in the meantime. In the UK gilt market, for example, investors at the time of writing could buy the Exchequer 10.5% stock 2005 at a price which produced a gross running yield of 8.65%, although capital depreciation over the period to maturity would be in the region of 20%.

Conversion of capital into income may be a logical decision for an elderly person with an estate in excess of the inheritance tax threshold, whose heirs would bear tax at 40% on the excess. This goes somewhat against conventional wisdom, which often recommends that retirees fix their income by investing in long-term bonds, even though these are known to be more volatile.

Are you a low or high rate taxpayer?

Tax considerations can dictate the choice of bond that is the best value. Newspapers like the *Financial Times* periodically publish information on the best value bonds for low rate and top rate taxpayers, reflecting the fact that capital gains on UK government bonds are exempt from CGT.

Investing in bonds through tax-free savings vehicles such as ISAs may be an interesting option for high rate taxpayers with no immediate need for income. Tax-free reinvestment of interest should produce a powerful compounding effect. As noted in Chapter 10 on collective investment in bonds, investors need to beware of the charges that some of these funds attract, and which can negate part of the tax benefit.

Do you want inflation proofing?

Index-linked government bonds have been a feature of some markets (including the USA and UK) for some time. They provide a fixed return over and above a specified benchmark such as the RPI. In the UK, which has the longest experience of dealing in such instruments, index-linked gilts tend to do best when there are fears of inflation rising. They often, therefore, move in a way contrary to the conventional gilt market.

Are you tolerant of volatility?

The section on duration in Chapter 2 made the point that longer term bonds are more volatile than shorter term, and low coupon bonds are more volatile than higher coupon. This means that investors can use the choice of bond to accommodate their tolerance of volatility to the purposes for which the bonds are being bought.

Investors believing interest rates are in a long-term downtrend may wish to buy long-term bonds with a low coupon, since their long duration means they are most responsive to interest rate movements. Those using bonds to reduce risk and enhance income in their portfolio may opt for bonds with a higher coupon, shorter maturity, and hence a relatively short duration.

In short, you can use bonds in ways that will accommodate most investment strategies. Many investors tend to overcomplicate their decisions and ignore the impact of transaction costs. You can buy gilts cheaply through the Post Office, and in the USA retail investors can use a similar direct dealing service with the US Treasury.

You can attain simple portfolio diversification by buying a spread of medium dated bonds with part of your capital and investing the rest in a low-cost share index tracker, making use of tax-free wrappers such as ISAs as appropriate. You can adjust the degree of risk involved by tailoring the percentages involved. A conservative strategy might have a 60% bond component, a less conservative one a 65/35 split in favour of the share index fund. It need be no more complicated than that.

IN BRIEF

- Most UK stockbrokers will deal in gilts. More esoteric bond choices may necessitate dealing through a bond specialist. Some online brokers deal only in shares.

- Choose any broker carefully, if necessary with a personal visit to the firm's offices. Make sure you choose the type of service right for you, and that you are aware of all the likely charges.

- Dealing in bonds has its own vocabulary. You need to be familiar with it before you begin dealing. All UK gilts have 'ticker' codes, just like shares.

- Online dealing in US bonds is much better developed. UK residents wishing to do this can open an account fairly easily.

- You can use spread betting in government bond futures for short-term speculation in government bond futures. You need to open a separate account with a spread-betting firm to do this.

- You can use bonds to accommodate a varied range of portfolio objectives in conjunction with shares or equity index-tracking funds.

chapter five

Investing in government bonds

Most investors who buy bonds deal in those issued by their own government, but the choice does not end there. Some broking firms allow clients to trade in the US bond market. This means that alert bond investors need to be aware of the characteristics of more than one market. In Europe too the advent of the Euro removed an obstacle to continental investors dealing in the bonds of other European governments.

This chapter looks at the government bond markets in the UK, USA, Euro-zone and Japan. It examines the background and history of the markets, their credit status, and how the markets are governed and regulated. It also looks at their structure, the ease with which private investors can deal in them, local bond and interest rate derivatives markets, and at some sources of information available to ordinary investors.

UK government bonds

Gilt-edge securities, or 'gilts', are UK government bonds. They are so called because the stock certificates that investors received were edged in gold leaf. But despite their evocative name, gilts are no different to any other government bonds. Because of its long history, the gilt market had some idiosyncratic features. In recent years, these have gradually been removed. There have been a number of reforms designed to bring the market into line with other leading government bond markets, chief among which have been: the creation of a group of well-capitalized primary dealers in the market (known as gilt-edge market makers or GEMMs) in place of the previously undercapitalized brokers who dealt in gilts; the creation of a repo market; the creation of a strips market; electronic settlement of gilt-edge deals; the granting of

> Despite their evocative name, gilts are no different to any other government bonds.

independence from government control to the Bank of England, under whose aegis the market operates (Table 5.1).

Repo (short for repurchase agreement) trading is a form of collateralized lending between dealers, designed to improve the liquidity of the market. Before this, lending and borrowing of stock occurred through the medium of a closed shop of so-called money brokers. It was a patently inefficient and opaque system at odds with the way these markets operated elsewhere.

> **Repo (short for repurchase agreement) trading is a form of collateralized lending between dealers.**

The introduction of a strips market allows gilts to be separated into their respective 'interest only' and 'principal only' components. This is primarily for use by market professionals. We'll look at how this works in more detail in the next chapter. This change also brought the gilt market into line with its US and continental counterparts. Private investors can deal in gilts in stripped form, although they should seek professional advice before doing so.

Bank of England independence has removed the direction of monetary policy – a big influence over the bond market – from overt political control. The Bank's monetary policy committee (MPC) now governs interest rate policy. Its members include both Bank of England officials and independent outside experts.

Electronic settlement of gilts was initially introduced a few years ago with the creation of the Central Gilt Office. This settlement system has now been absorbed by CREST, which was hitherto an equities settlement system. The Bank of England underwrote and launched it in the wake of the failure of the Stock Exchange's Taurus project. The merging of CREST and the CGO has centralized settlement of all securities trading in the UK in one system.

UK government securities have long been rated AAA by leading credit rating agencies. The characteristics of gilt-edge stocks are similar to government bonds issued in other markets. Today stocks are usually

Table 5.1 How the gilt market was modernized

- Creation of GEMMs
- Creation of repo market
- Creation of strippable gilts
- Creation of CGO
- Bank of England independence

issued with the designation 'Treasury Stock'. In the past 'Exchequer', 'Funding', 'Conversion' and certain other terms were used. These remain in force for some stocks currently traded. The labels have no practical significance.

By convention the market categorizes UK government bonds according to the number of years left to maturity. This differs from the USA, where the market uses the number of years to maturity at the time of issue. In the UK, gilts are 'short dated' if they have less than seven years to run to maturity, 'medium dated' if they fall into the 7–15 year band, and 'long dated' if they have 15 or more years to go until they are redeemed. There are also a small number of irredeemable stocks, which are stocks that have no maturity date.

Most gilts pay fixed coupons on a twice-yearly basis and are 'bullets'. This means they repay the principal amount in full in a single payment on maturity. However, several other types of bond exist. These include: those that offer an option to convert a short-dated bond into one of longer maturity; dual redemption date bonds, which allow the government to redeem the bond at any time between the two dates; and index-linked bonds, where interest payments and redemption value are linked to the retail price index. We'll look at index-linked bonds in more detail in Chapter 8.

The Treasury's Debt Management Office (DMO) issues gilts largely through an auction process. This allows primary dealers (the GEMMs) to make competitive bids for new gilt issues, which are then distributed through them to investors. This is similar to the US system. The rules require GEMMs to bid at auctions and to make constant two-way prices in all gilt-edge stock. GEMMs also deal with each other on an anonymous basis through a small number of Inter Dealer Brokers (IDBs). This allows market makers to conduct hedging and book squaring trades without disclosing sensitive information to other market participants. The Debt Management Office sometimes also issues smaller tranches of existing gilts through a tender system.

The market recently moved from pricing in thirty-seconds and sixty-fourths to a decimal pricing basis, and the basis for calculating accrued interest has now moved to an actual/actual basis rather than, as was the case before, an actual/365 basis. From a taxation standpoint, interest on gilts often used to be paid net of tax although it was always possible to receive it gross. With self-assessment, many investors now elect to receive gilt interest gross, although it must still be declared for tax at the appropriate time. Interest can be paid direct to a bank account. Capital gains on gilts are tax free. This means that low coupon stocks, where the capital gain may make up a higher proportion of the return, tend to be favoured by higher rate taxpayers. It also means that the capital uplift arising in index-linked stocks is also free of tax. Transactions in gilts are also free of stamp duty. LIFFE offers traders one major contract on the gilt-edge market, the long gilt future. The underlying is a notional bond with a 7% coupon. It also offers a short-term contract based on a three-month bill.

S I D E B A R

How bond futures work

Futures based around interest rates and bonds work in two main ways. Short-term interest rate contracts, such as LIFFE's 'short sterling' contract, mimic a short-term bill. They are priced at a discount that reflects the prevailing short-term interest rate. So if the market expects that the benchmark interest rate at the time the future comes up for delivery will be 4%, the future would, in simple terms, be priced at 96 (100–4). If expectations changed and the market expected interest rates to fall to 3.5%, the price of the future would rise to 96.5.

LIFFE's 'long gilt' futures contract is similar to those of other markets. Long-term bond futures are generally constructed around a notional bond with a known coupon and specified maturity bracket. The contract is in effect a hybrid of a number of actual bonds. Any one of these bonds or a basket of them can be delivered against the future. In the case of the LIFFE contract, for example, the bonds have to have a single maturity date between 8.75 and 13 years away from the delivery month of the contract.

At any one time one particular bond will mathematically be the 'cheapest to deliver' against the future. Considerable effort and sophistication goes into calculating which bond is likely to fulfil this requirement.

One advantage that the futures market provides is the ability it offers professional bond traders to 'hedge'. This means they can insure against an adverse price movement in the underlying market by using an off setting transaction in the futures market.

More prosaically, bond futures prices are also an effective gauge of where 'the market' expects both short-term interest rates and long-term bond yields to be at the time a particular futures contract expires. At the time of writing the March 2002 short sterling future was priced at 94.74, suggesting that at the time, the market expected short-term interest rates to be 5.26%.

Information on the gilt market is available at a variety of sources. These include newspapers like the *Financial Times* and weekly publications such as the *Investors Chronicle*. Prices of gilt-edge stock are shown daily on the capital markets page of the FT. The *Weekend Money* section of the Saturday FT has a variety of other information of interest to bond investors. This information includes the stocks that appear to offer the best value for different categories of taxpayer.

On the web, Bloomberg (www.bloomberg.co.uk) is a good all-round source for information on the bond markets. The Debt Management Office website (www.dmo.gov.uk) has exhaustive background data on the market. This includes annual reviews, a calendar of forthcoming issues and a range of other information. Sources of bond market information are dealt with in more detail in Chapter 9.

US government bonds

Fancy lending money to the US government? Just open a dollar account with a leading broker like Charles Schwab or CSFBDirect, and you can do so. You do this through the simple expedient of buying a US Treasury bond. The US bond market is huge and actively traded, larger than any other single

> **Fancy lending money to the US government?**

country's. It may eventually come to be rivalled in size by the market in Euro-zone government bonds. But for the moment it is unchallenged. Not only that, in addition to Treasury securities there are a number of other issues in the US bond market that are popular with investors and have quasi-government status. These include bonds issued by agencies such as FNMA and GNMA (government backed mortgage lenders), and those of cities and municipalities. The latter are popular with investors because of their tax-free status.

The US market provides the benchmark for the rest of the world. Government bonds in all other jurisdictions are typically measured in terms of the difference in yield (or 'spread') between them and the comparable US Treasury bond. One reason the US government bond market is so big has been the past predilection of the US government for running fiscal deficits, which have to be financed somewhere. That somewhere has typically been the bond market.

The US is a benchmark in other ways too. The structure of the market and the instruments it offers have been widely copied in other markets. This is particularly true of innovations such as the repo market and the market for strippable bonds (as described previously). The only main exception is that the UK led the way in the creation of an index-linked bond market in 1981. It was followed by the USA only in 1997.

The Federal Reserve (known universally as the Fed) controls monetary policy and the issuing of government securities. The Fed is the US central bank. It operates through its HQ in Washington and via a network of regional offices. The most important of these (from the standpoint of the bond market) is based in New York. The Fed is perceived to be independent although, as some observers point out, its chairman and board of governors are appointed by the incumbent administration, and their appointments ratified by Congress. In addition the Fed chairman is frequently called to testify to congressional committees. The Fed's official objectives are to maintain price stability and employment, although some might say that its role has expanded to include maintaining the general level of the stock market.

Despite what in other countries might be viewed as a rather profligate approach to public finances, and periodic large budget deficits notwith-standing, US Treasury securities are rated AAA by leading credit rating agencies (Figure 5.1).

The structure of the US market is fundamentally the same as most other government bond markets. As with other bond markets, there are some differences in terminology. The US market has a three-tier structure:

1. Treasury bills are issued for maturities up to a year. They are sold on the basis of a discounted price rather than a coupon.

2. Treasury notes are issued with a maturity of 1–10 years and have fixed coupons paid semi-annually, with the principal repaid as a single 'bullet' at maturity.

3. Treasury bonds have a maturity of 10–30 years but otherwise have the same characteristics as Treasury notes.

In early 2001 the Fed announced that it was planning changes to the market, designed to rationalize its structure and concentrate liquidity into slightly fewer instruments. As explained in Chapter 3, as part of these changes the 30-year bond (known as the 'long bond') may be phased out. This is a surprising move in view of its status as a benchmark, and the consequent active trading it enjoys.

The Fed issues Treasury bonds, notes and bills with reasonable pre-dictability. Issues of two-year and five-year notes occur monthly, ten-year notes four times a year, and long-term bonds twice yearly. Government bond sales are always auctions. Primary dealers (usually the large investment banks) are the major participants in the market.

As is the case in other countries, primary dealers gain certain privileges

Figure 5.1 US Treasury benchmark yield curve

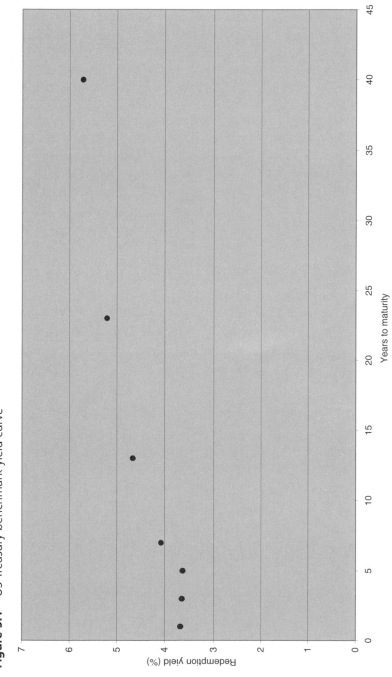

for the obligations they undertake. These include preferential access at auctions and direct access to the Fed trading room.

Interest on Treasuries is paid gross and prices are quoted 'clean', with no adjustment made for accrued interest. Accrued interest is calculated on an actual/actual basis and bondholders may opt for settlement either in book entry or certificated form. Pricing is now on a decimal basis. Trading in US Treasuries in the secondary market is conducted on a round-the-clock basis and is international in scope.

There is an active derivatives market in Chicago, which covers a considerable part of the US Treasury maturity spectrum. The Chicago Board of Trade (CBOT) is particularly noted for its trading of a Treasury bond future (for maturities of 15 years and up). It has futures contracts on the ten-year bond, and five-year and two-year notes. It lists options on all of the above. Shorter term interest rate futures are mainly traded at the Chicago Mercantile Exchange (CME).

> **Access to the bond market is relatively easy for US investors.**

Access to the bond market is relatively easy for US investors. Most brokers offer online dealing in a variety of bonds. Private investors are

---

S I D E B A R

On-the-run versus off-the-run: a cautionary tale

The most recently issued bonds tend to be the most liquid. They are known as 'on-the-run' bonds. Yields on 'off-the-run' bonds tend to be slightly higher, even though their terms are similar to the benchmark.

One popular trade conducted by the now notorious Long Term Capital Management (LTCM) was to arbitrage or exploit tiny price differences between the on-the-run and off-the-run bonds, selling short the former and buying the latter on the grounds that their yields would ultimately converge.

A contributory factor to the fund's demise was that the flight to quality after the Russian default in August 1998 led to a surge in price of the more liquid on-the-run bonds that LTCM had borrowed to sell short, and depressed the price of the less liquid bonds the fund held. This meant sizeable short-term losses.

The moral of the story: in times of crisis it is the most liquid bonds, not the cheapest, which investors favour.

frequent traders in government, agency, municipal and corporate bonds. This reflects the greater knowledge and sophistication of the US private investor. Non-US private investors can gain access to this market by opening an account with a local broker, wiring funds and filling in a non-resident tax declaration. Non-residents must use the services of a local custodian. Their broker will probably provide this service (for a fee). UK residents can receive interest income from US Treasury bonds free of tax. In addition, investors intending to buy bonds and hold them to maturity can also buy cheaply and easily through Treasury Direct. This is a service operated by the Fed for small investors.

Day-to-day information on the US Treasury market is contained in most US-based financial newspapers, notably the *Wall Street Journal*. Web-based bond information is available on the excellent Bloomberg site (www.bloomberg.com). It has prices for the most liquid securities and bond-related news.

In addition the Bureau of Public Debt (www.publicdebt.treas.gov) has commission-free dealing (for US residents). It also has a considerable amount of information relating to the market, as does Long Bond (www.longbond.com). The Federal Reserve's own site (www.federalreserve.gov) contains a wide range of information about the economy and the bond market.

Euro-zone government bonds

Although individual Euro-zone countries still issue bonds in their own name, to all intents and purposes the market is gradually becoming a unified one. This is more so since it now has a common monetary policy administered through the European Central Bank (ECB). The locking of Euro-zone exchange rates has meant yield curves are increasingly similar in all countries. Any differences are the result of small variations in perceptions over credit quality between different governments.

Table 5.2 Some European government bond names

Country	Names used
UK	Gilts
France	OATs, BTANs, BTFs
Germany	Bunds, Bobl, Buxl
Italy	BTPs, BOTs, CCTs, CTZs

New bond issues from Euro-zone governments are now being made solely in Euros. This development should, in turn, bind the market together even more in the future. It will give the market a size that rivals that of US Treasury securities. The denomination of government debt issued before the advent of the Euro has been converted from local currencies into Euros.

At the outset of monetary union, Italy, Germany and France together accounted for 76% of the bond issues outstanding, with the Netherlands and Belgium together making up a further 14%. Bond investing has a long history in Italy and Germany. That said, the larger individual country bond markets have kept many of their distinct features and are worth considering separately in turn.

France

The French government bond market has long been one of the more liquid in Europe. This has not occurred by accident. Since the 1980s the French Treasury has pursued a single-minded strategy to make it so. It has done this through offering a range of simple and highly liquid products that appeal to specific categories of investor and through making new bond issues in a predictable and consistent manner. There have been various other market innovations. There are several examples. France issued long-term, ECU-denominated bonds in 1989 and had a regular programme of ECU issues from 1994 onwards. It has also been active in providing information to intermediaries, investors and analysts.

Like the USA, the French government bond market has a relatively simple three-tier structure, with bills, shorter term notes and long-term bonds. French debt is rated AAA by leading credit rating agencies.

The acronym BTF (Bons du Trésor à taux fixé et à intérêt précompte) denotes short-term bonds. The term translates as fixed rate bonds with pre-calculated interest (i.e. issued at a discount). BTANs (Bons du Trésor à taux fixé et à intérêt annuel) are medium dated bonds with a maturity of two to five years. OATs (Obligations assimilables du Trésor) are longer term bonds with either fixed or index-linked coupons and with interest also paid annually. BTANs and OATs are auctioned on a monthly basis using a competitive auction system. Primary dealers, brokers and other inter-mediaries can bid on an equal footing, although primary dealers account for 90% of the market.

Three factors add to the liquidity of the market. One is that the government has a policy of issuing debt that is identical to existing issues and therefore interchangeable ('fungible' in bond market jargon) with it. This enhances liquidity. In addition there are incentives for primary market makers to keep the market liquid. Finally, the government operates a debt management fund. While remaining neutral overall, the fund can intervene from to time in the market to aid liquidity.

OATs are listed on the Paris bourse, but other issues trade on an over-the-counter basis. Stocks are in bearer form and normally held within the Euroclear/Cedel (now called Clearstream) settlement systems. There is no withholding tax for non-resident holders of the bonds. The Paris financial market was among the first in Europe to develop the concepts of a repo market and strippable bonds.

Derivatives based around French bonds are mainly confined to a single contract, the 'Notionnel'. In the past this has been one of the most actively traded bond futures in the world. It is based around a notional 7–10 year bond. A future on a longer term (15-year) bond has also been traded in the past, but much less actively.

> **The Paris financial market was among the first in Europe to develop the concepts of a repo market and strippable bonds.**

Germany

In the period prior to monetary union, German government bonds were the continent's blue chips. This status stemmed from the formidable reputation for independence possessed by the Bundesbank, its overriding goal of maintaining the value of the D-Mark, and its obsession with minimizing inflation. In a de facto sense the German market is still first among equals. German bond yields are the benchmark against which other Euro-zone bonds are measured. Although the functions of the Bundesbank have been subsumed into the ECB, its location in Frankfurt suggests that German monetary discipline remains at the heart of Euro-zone policy making.

Germany's bond market is more complicated than most because of the country's federal structure and because the German government, either officially or unofficially, guarantees the bonds of a range of other institutions. These include the Bundesbahn, Bundespost and other federal entities, as well as various regional organizations including mortgage banks (the so-called Pfandebriefe). These are akin to the GMNA and FNMA guarantees that operate in the USA.

Pfandebriefe bonds typically offer higher yields than conventional government bonds of the same maturity, but effectively carry the imprint of the German government. Background on the Pfandebriefe market is available at www.pfandebriefe.org.

Bond maturities in Germany range from four to 30 years with the mainstream bonds, known as Bunds (Bundesanleihen), generally having a ten-year life. The government also issues shorter dated bonds known as

Bobls (Bundesobligationen). These usually have maturities of four to five years. From time to time the government has also issued extra long-term Bunds (known in the market as BUXLs) when demand warrants it.

Unlike the systematic French system of formalized bond issues and policies to concentrate liquidity, in Germany the issues are less structured. There are Bund issues every month, but often no formal schedule. The issue mechanism is also less transparent. Two tranches are usually issued. The first is at a fixed price to a syndicate headed by the Bundesbank, which typically retains a portion of the issue for day-to-day market intervention purposes. The second tranche is auctioned in much the same way as in other markets (Table 5.3).

Other idiosyncratic features of the German bond market include an accrued interest count based on a 30/360 basis as distinct from the actual/actual used in France, the UK and USA. Under this convention each month is assumed to have 30 days. Interest on German bonds is also only paid after deduction of 30% withholding tax. This is something of a bugbear for German bond fans; particularly given the temptations offered by effectively tax-free bearer Eurobonds and the proximity of safety deposit boxes in Luxembourg.

Derivatives based around the Bund used to be the preserve of London's LIFFE exchange, but the British contract gradually lost ground to its counterpart in Frankfurt. This was partly because LIFFE was slow to abandon floor trading. Frankfurt's futures exchange (now part of the combined German-Swiss Eurex exchange) had always been an electronic market. Trading in the Bund contract is now firmly based at Eurex. Ironically, LIFFE does appear to have snagged most of the trade in short-term derivatives contracts based around Euro-zone interest rates.

Table 5.3 Comparison of main Euro-zone bond markets

	France	*Germany*	*Italy*
Size (bn EUR)	528	565	574
Issue method	Auction	Mixed	Dutch auction
Accrued interest	A/A	30/360	A/A
Withholding tax	No	Yes	Yes
Maturity spectrum	2–30	4–30	3–30
Index linked	Yes	No	No
Strips	Yes	Yes	Yes
Repo	Yes	No	No
Derivative	Notionnel	Bund future	BTP future
Where traded	Paris	Eurex	LIFFE

Italy

Holders of Italian government bonds had a welcome bonanza a few years back. They benefited in a big way from the so-called 'convergence rally' that took place when it became clear that the Euro would launch on schedule. Hitherto its bonds had been trading on a credit rating a notch below AAA. As a consequence, at the time Italian bonds yielded appreciably more than Bunds.

Italian political instability had always been the Achilles heel of its bond market when it came to attracting foreign investors, but domestic ones, especially retail investors, were generally happy to support it. The Italian bond market is not, however, without its own idiosyncratic touches. About a quarter of the public debt remains in ultra-short-term bonds – BOTs (Buoni Ordinari del Tesoro), issued at a discount with maturities ranging out to 12 months.

BTPs (Buoni del Tesoro Poliennali) have been the most popular form of bond investment, particularly among foreign investors. These are straight bonds paying a semi-annual coupon. They are typically issued in three-, five- and ten-year maturities, with an occasional 30-year issue.

There are several other variants. CCTs are longer maturity bonds (typically around seven years). The difference is that they have some inflation protection built in, albeit by means of a complicated formula and with a quirky payment structure. More recent issues have had simpler terms, to make them easier to sell to investors.

The government has also issued zero-coupon bonds (CTZs), which have proved particularly popular with retail investors. They are popular with the government too. Because they are issued at a deep discount and pay no interest, they appear to reduce the government's overall interest bill.

Italian government bond interest payments are normally subject to a 12.5% withholding tax. Overseas holders are exempt from this and can either be reimbursed, or the tax not levied in the first place. Bonds are sold via a Dutch auction system and in consecutive slices to ensure each issue remains liquid.

Derivatives are available in the more liquid parts of the market, notably through LIFFE's long-established BTP future, first launched in 1991.

Euro-zone bond information

Local financial newspapers remain the best primary source of information on individual Euro-zone bond markets. The *Financial Times* capital markets page has a good summary of their principal features and instruments. Bloomberg (www.bloomberg.co.uk) has benchmark bond prices and yields for German, French and Italian bonds. Barclays Capital also maintains some statistical information on Euro government bond markets (www.barclayscapital.com).

Japanese government bonds

Anyone who has visited Japan will know that it is different: the same is true of its bond market. A lengthy period of recession and price deflation has resulted in yields on government bonds falling to microscopic levels.

> Anyone who has visited Japan will know that it is different: the same is true of its bond market.

Japanese government bonds (JGBs) are issued across a relatively wide spectrum of maturities, including two-, three- and four-year bonds. There are also five-year bonds issued as discount (rather than coupon-bearing). The most frequently issued, however, is a 10-year bond. There have also been issues as short as six years and as long as 20 years in the longer term category. Fixed coupon bonds tend to be of the familiar western form with semi-annual interest payments and single bullet maturity.

In round numbers the size of the bond market is some JPY360trn, of which almost exactly half is long-term JGBs. A further JPY100m is split roughly two-thirds/one-third between 2 to 6-year maturities and those of less than one year. Bonds issued by government agencies and public sector bodies make up the balance. Credit rating agencies rate JGBs as ΛΛΛ. This is partly because of Japan's position as a leading global creditor nation and partly because of a highly advanced and well-diversified economy.

Issues occur primarily through two methods. One involves a widely dispersed syndicate of professional investors, approximately 2000 in number. A typical issue entails the larger part of the issue being auctioned to syndicate members. The remainder is sold in the market but under-written by the syndicate. Unlike other markets, there is no obligation on syndicate members to make a market in the bonds following an issue. This is a significant difference between the Japanese bond market and those of other countries.

Aside from the syndicate method, bonds are sold at public auction, primarily although not exclusively to professional investors. Bonds are in registered or bearer form and interest is subject to a withholding tax. Accrued interest on Japanese bonds is calculated on an actual/365 basis. A repo market operates in JGBs. As yet there has been no development of a strips market. Futures on the 10-year JGB are traded at LIFFE and at some other futures exchanges. The future is based around a notional long-term bond with a 6% coupon.

Despite its size, roughly three times the size of the German bond market and second only to US Treasuries, the JGB market is illiquid. The exception is the benchmark 10-year issue, which is the basis for actively traded futures contracts. Because of this, international bond investors dislike the market. This is despite the country's negligible inflation, which would otherwise be favourable to bond investment.

The government is aware of the criticism and recently took steps to improve matters. It announced it would discontinue four- and six-year bonds and merge these into existing five-year issues. In addition the system whereby international investors can gain exemption from withholding tax is being simplified. From now on, bonds held by foreign investors in the accounts of large global custodians will normally be exempt from the tax as a matter of course.

For ordinary western investors, information on JGBs is sparse. Prices for JGB futures are listed in the *Financial Times*, as are yields and spreads on JGBs alongside information on other government bonds. The Japanese Ministry of Finance (www.mof.go.jp) has a certain amount of information available at its website. This includes a quarterly newsletter that contains a considerable amount of information on the market. The ubiquitous Bloomberg site also has a page devoted to JGB prices and yields and carries news relevant to bond investing in Japan.

Unlike the markets described earlier, accessibility to the market is virtually non-existent for private investors in the west.

Other markets

The preceding sections have covered the characteristics of the main government bond markets. For retail investors, access to markets other than their own is in practice restricted to the ability to open a dollar account with the US broker and deal in US Treasuries and other similar bonds.

In theory, Euro-zone investors ought to be able to deal in the instruments of other Euro-zone governments with little difficulty. In practice, however, there is little incentive for them do to so. This is because yields have converged so much: transaction costs and the hassle factor probably more than offset any remaining yield advantage to be gained from shopping around.

As an indication of the pecking order, Table 5.4 shows the yield spread versus US Treasuries (widely seen as the benchmark) of government bonds in various jurisdictions both inside and outside the Euro-zone.

Table 5.4 European 10-year benchmark government bonds

Country	Yield %	Spread vs US Treasuries (bp)
Austria	5.32	5
Belgium	5.28	1
Denmark	5.24	−3
Finland	5.24	−3
France	5.16	−11
Germany	5.00	−27
Greece	5.49	−22
Ireland	5.28	1
Italy	5.39	12
Netherlands	5.15	−12
Norway	6.29	102
Portugal	5.39	12
Spain	5.29	2
Sweden	5.05	−22
Switzerland	3.44	−183
UK	5.18	−9

Source: Financial Times

These spreads say interesting things about the perceptions of investors. Italy is seen as less risky than Greece, and rightly so. But based on past history the gap might be deemed too narrow. Government bond investors, especially the professionals, need to make fine judgements on the basis of these figures. It's probably fair to say that they earn their money.

I N   B R I E F

■ Most investors confine their bond buying to government bonds.

■ Government bond markets in most developed markets are fundamentally similar in structure, although some have their idiosyncrasies.

■ For UK investors, the gilt market offers a wide variety of stocks to deal in. UK investors can also gain fairly easy access to the US bond market through online brokers.

■ Euro-zone government bond yields have converged dramatically. It is scarcely worthwhile investors in government bonds straying from their own market.

■ One exception is the bonds issued by quasi-governmental organizations in Germany (especially local mortgage banks). These carry an unofficial government guarantee yet have higher yields than conventional government bonds.

■ The Japanese government bond market is inaccessible to western private investors.

Bond market oddities

S o far in this book we have made the general assumption that the bonds mentioned are 'straight' bonds; that is, they have a fixed coupon paid once or twice a year and are redeemed in full on a single date in the future. Most bonds do conform to this stereotype. However, a significant minority have different characteristics. This affects how they are valued, and the types of investor for which they might be suitable.

Typical jargon phrases used to describe bonds like this include: linkers, floaters, FRNs, TIPS, strips, zeros, extendibles, retractables, convertibles, exchangeables and irredeemables. The jargon boils down into six distinct genres, which we'll look at in turn, namely:

- index-linked bonds
- floating rate notes
- zero-coupon bonds
- convertible bonds
- undated bonds
- other oddities.

The distinction between these bonds and their more 'normal' cousins is that, in contrast to 'straight' bonds, these variants usually have one or more of the key bond components either absent or adjusted, or else some new features added.

These differences are briefly as follows. With index-linked bonds, interest and maturity value are linked to movements in inflation. With zeros, there is no coupon. Floating rate notes have a fixed maturity date and value, but a coupon which floats with the general level of interest rates. Extendibles and retractables have a variable maturity date. Undated or irredeemable bonds have a fixed coupon but no redemption date.

Convertible bonds are effectively 'straight' bonds with an inbuilt option to switch into a fixed number of shares in the issuer at a predetermined price. Exchangeables are like convertibles, but where the option is to switch into the shares of a company other than the issuer (Table 6.1).

It's worth pointing out that each of these types of bonds is common to most bond markets, whether government bonds, Eurobonds or corporate bonds. Bond markets in all jurisdictions have one or other of the variants. Each market does, however, put its particular spin in the terms and conditions under which such bonds work, and their tax treatment. So if you invest outside your home market, check up on any differences first. Don't assume that they work in other markets in exactly the way you're used to.

Table 6.1 Oddball bonds summarized

Name	Coupon	Maturity	Other feature
Index linked	Indexed	Fixed	Principal indexed
FRN	Floating	Fixed	Based on reference rate
Zero	None	Fixed	Issued at deep discount
Irredeemable	Yes	None	
Convertible	Fixed	Fixed	Built-in call option

Index-linked

Index-linked government bonds adjust principal and interest to allow for the effects of inflation. The UK was a pioneer of this concept. The first index-linked gilts were issued in 1981 under the auspices of Nigel (now Lord) Lawson. Since that time others have followed suit. The US Treasury issued TIPS (Treasury Inflation Proofed Securities) in 10- and 30-year maturities in January 1997. France also has inflation proofed OATs (see the previous chapter on government bond markets for an explanation of OATs), known as OATis. Other countries with a sizeable index-linked government bond market include Israel, Sweden, Canada and Australia. The UK market is by far the largest.

> if you invest outside your home market, check up on any differences first. Don't assume that they work in other markets in exactly the way you're used to.

Although index-linked bonds are normally taken to mean linked to inflation, in fact they can be linked to any index. It would be possible to index a bond to a broad equity market index, although this would probably defeat the objective: to provide secure inflation proofed income and capital with a modest return on top. Yields on index-linked gilts have recently been in the region of 2% adjusted for inflation.

How index-linked bonds work varies from country to country. In the UK, the inflation protection is achieved by adjusting the value of principal for inflation each time a coupon payment is made. So for a stock that pays a coupon twice yearly, as most gilts do, the adjustment takes place every six months. The adjustment factor is calculated by reference to the original nominal value of the holding at issue and the RPI at time of issue and the present. The coupon is paid on the uplifted capital value. The result is indirectly to index-link the interest payments and of course the principal. To be more precise, the RPI factor is actually taken eight months in arrears. Table 6.2 shows the information you need and how to use it to calculate interest payments and redemption values. To simplify things, the example uses a fictional index-linked bond with RPI adjustments six months in arrears.

Table 6.2 Valuing index-linked stocks: example

Government of Ruritania 5% index-linked stock 2012 (issued 1 Jan 2001)

Interest payment dates: 30 June and 31 December

Calculation basis for index: RPI six months previously

Assume RPI at end June 2001 was 103 (30 June 2000 = 100)

Calculating interest payments

Coupon paid in December 2001 = 2.5 × 100 × 103/100 = 2.575 per 100 nominal

(*working*: coupon times nominal value adjusted for change between RPI six months before issue date and six months before coupon payment date)

Calculating redemption value

Assume inflation is 2.5% per year until redemption date

RPI six months prior to redemption date will be 185.39

Redemption value is therefore 185.39 per 100 nominal

It's important to point out several other important features of index-linked bonds (Table 6.3). The first is that the guarantee relates to the nominal value of the bond you buy. If you pay above par and hold to maturity, as with any normal bond you will suffer a loss of capital value. In the case of an index-linked bond, the loss will be notional, because inflation will probably more than make up the difference, but you need to remember this point when working out how much you will get back when the bond matures.

Table 6.3 Key features of index-linked bonds

- Guaranteed based on nominal value
- Inflation protection not exact
- Inflation adjustment down as well as up
- Yields lower than comparable conventional stock
- Low liquidity
- Redemption yield calculations require assumptions
- CGT advantages for higher rate taxpayers

Second, because of the time lag in adjusting for inflation, the protection offered is not exact. This may or may not be beneficial. At a time when inflation is falling rapidly, index-linked yields can look attractive in the short term, because the adjustment factor is backward looking. By the same token 'inflation scares' are good for sentiment towards index-linked bonds, even though the inflation protection takes time to catch up.

The third point to bear in mind – especially in an era when the fear is of deflation rather than inflation – is that the adjustment factor works both ways. If inflation is negative (i.e. the RPI falls for a sustained period), the redemption value and interest payments on index-linked stocks will be adjusted downwards. At least this is what happens with index-linked gilts.

While this absence of a floor may seem of little consequence to those brought up in the post-war era of rapid inflation, it is worth remembering that long periods of sustained price deflation have been a feature of economic history. Prices fell substantially in the first half of the thirteenth century, for much of the nineteenth century and in the 1930s. At times like this, conventional bonds, not index linked, would have proved the best investments.

Fourth, remember that index-linked yields are not the same as real yields. The real yield on a conventional 10-year gilt is calculated by subtracting the inflation rate from the redemption yield. A 10-year, index-linked gilt will normally have a redemption yield less than the real yield on a conventional gilt with the same maturity. The reason for this is that index-linked yields compensate not just for actual inflation, but for any eventuality on the inflation front for as long as the investor holds them. This certainty has a price, which is reflected in the lower yields. There is, in other words, a risk premium present in the higher real yields on conventional gilts.

Fifth, most investors hold stocks like this to maturity. This particularly applies to professional investors at pension funds, where index-linked gilts are used to guarantee future pension liabilities. Because of this, trading in index-linked gilt stocks is relatively thin and dealing spreads may be wider than in conventional stocks.

Sixth, redemption yields on index-linked stocks can only be worked out by making specific assumptions about future rates of inflation. Tables of yields on index-linked stocks in the *Financial Times*, for example, assume inflation at a consistent 2.5% and 5% a year and work out separate yields on each of these two bases.

Finally, in the UK index-linked gilts are perceived to have particular advantages for higher rate taxpayers. The reason is that not only are capital gains on gilts exempt from CGT, but so also is the inflation protection element in the coupon. Tax is only payable on the (relatively low) coupon payment based on nominal value. In reality though, because index-linked returns are relatively low, many investors would be better off with higher coupon non-index-linked stocks, even if it means paying additional tax.

What index-linked stocks are on offer? Table 6.4 shows the maturity date, coupon, issue size and ticker symbol for the UK index-linked gilts currently in issue.

As you can see from Table 6.4, UK index-linked stocks cover the full maturity spectrum. There are sizeable amounts of each stock in issue, but much of it is, in market jargon, 'tightly held'. This illiquidity does not, however, usually cause a major problem for private investors dealing in modest amounts.

Other than the tax considerations, index-linked stocks have attractions for any investor wishing to have a fixed return inflation proofed. The usual holders are pension funds, but index-linked bonds can be tax-efficient investment vehicles for higher rate taxpayers. Investors in countries with a history of low inflation typically display little interest in index-linked bonds.

Table 6.4   Index-linked gilts: dealing data

Issue	Coupon %	Maturity	Ticker	Issue size (£bn)
Treasury	2.5	2003	TR03	2.7
Treasury	4.375	2004	T04A	1.3
Treasury	2.5	2009	TR09	2.6
Treasury	2.5	2011	TR2H	3.5
Treasury	2.5	2013	T13I	4.6
Treasury	2.5	2016	TR16	4.9
Treasury	2.5	2020	T2HI	4.2
Treasury	2.5	2024	T24I	4.8
Treasury	4.125	2030	T30I	2.6

A relatively modest number of index-linked Treasury stock has been issued in the USA, linked to the CPI-U, the consumer price index for urban consumers. In Australia the government has issued TIBs (Treasury indexed bonds) in comparatively small amounts at longer maturities. Canada has real return bonds, linked to the consumer price index. These are somewhat along the same lines as the UK's index-linked stock, but with coupons only paid once a year.

In France the OATi market has proved popular. This has been especially true of bonds in the shorter of the two maturity areas. There is currently some EUR17.8bn in terms of market value outstanding in the 2009 maturities. These bonds have a coupon of 3%. About EUR3.6bn of market value is currently outstanding in the 2029 maturity. Here the coupon is 3.4%. OATis are single annual coupon bonds linked to French CPI. In the case of the 2009 series, the base date for indexing is 25 July 1998. 'Real' yields on OATis peaked at around 2% in November 1999 and at the time of writing were around 1.5%.

> **Index-linked securities should be avoided like the plague if deflation is in prospect.**

On the whole, governments like index-linked securities. One reason is that they are cheap (at least in the short term) in terms of interest and debt repayment costs. The investor population at large seems to like them too. From an investment standpoint they are best invested in at times when inflation is high but economic growth and therefore inflationary pressure is decelerating. They should be avoided like the plague if deflation is in prospect.

Floaters

Floating rate notes (FRNs) are unsecured medium to long-term bonds. The difference between FRNs and conventional bonds is that they do not have a fixed interest rate. Instead, the interest paid on the bonds varies, reflecting the movement in a particular benchmark, or reference, rate of interest. The reference rate used is one that is determined by supply and demand in the market rather than fixed by the central bank.

> **Floating rate notes (FRNs) are unsecured medium to long-term bonds.**

In the case of the UK, the common reference rate for FRNs is LIBOR. This is shorthand for London InterBank Offered Rate. In the USA a short-term Treasury bill rate is generally used. In the Euro-zone either LIBOR or EURIBOR (Euro InterBank Offered Rate) is used as a reference rate.

Interest on floating rate notes is generally paid either quarterly or half-yearly and is based on the rate on a particular 'fixing' day, subject to a minimum. The rate paid will be the reference rate plus or minus a pre-determined spread expressed in basis points. A basis point is one-hundredth of a percentage point. For example, if LIBOR is 5% and the terms of a floating rate note called for interest to be fixed at LIBOR plus 50bp (0.5%), the rate paid would 5.5%. If by the next fixing date LIBOR were 4.25%, the rate paid would be 4.75% – and so on down to the floor rate. If reference rates rise, the coupon payment rises in the same way (Figure 6.1).

The premium over LIBOR or any other reference rate used is determined by the credit quality of the issuer. The lower the credit quality of the issuer, the higher will be the premium over LIBOR of the FRN. FRNs are generally (although not always) issued by companies and so fall into the category broadly covered by corporate bonds.

The reason companies issue FRNs is often related to a takeover. The reasoning is as follows. The UK Takeover Code requires that if a company buys shares in another company which it later bids for, it must make an alternative offer in cash that is at least as high as the highest price it paid for shares bought prior to that takeover.

Bids are often made in the form of shares in the bidding company. In volatile markets or in bear markets, rational investors are equally likely, or more likely, to accept the cash alternative rather than an offer whose money value depends on the bidding company's share price.

The drawback to accepting a cash alternative is that it counts as a disposal for capital gains tax purposes, whereas swapping your target company shares for the bidder's does not. To accommodate shareholders who are already up to their CGT exemption, bidders therefore frequently offer the option for holders to receive the cash alternative in the form of a floating rate note. The FRN can then be sold gradually over a period of years and offset against allowable losses and CGT annual exemptions.

You are not forced to accept the FRN instead of the cash, but it will almost certainly help to ease your tax position if you do. The reason an FRN is better than cash, tax considerations aside, is that it will normally offer a rate of interest superior to an instant access bank deposit. Because the rate floats, the value of the FRN stays unchanged at par throughout its life.

In accepting a floating rate note offer, a holder is more or less guaranteed that it will be repaid at par. The only doubt, as outlined earlier, relates to the credit quality of the issuer. If it is perceived there is a chance of the issuer defaulting, perhaps because its balance sheet was already strained prior to the takeover, then investors should get a bigger premium over the reference rate. Whether or not the premium is sufficiently large to offset the credit doubts is a judgement investors must make for

Figure 6.1 Three-month LIBOR, 1996–2000

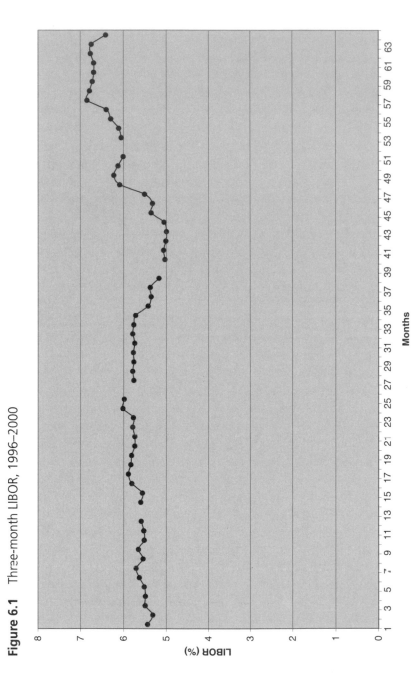

themselves. This issue will be explored in greater detail in Chapter 8, which covers corporate bonds.

Zeros

Zero-coupon bonds have all of the interest rolled up in the return of principal when the security matures. Issued at a deep discount to face value, their return is derived solely from the capital appreciation that results as they approach maturity.

At this point it is worth revisiting the section on duration in Chapter 2. A zero-coupon bond will have a longer duration than a conventional bonds with the same redemption date. Its duration will be identical to the length of its maturity. Zeros are therefore more sensitive to the prospect for interest rate movements during their life than a coupon-bearing bond of the same maturity.

Zero-coupon bonds date back to ideas developed in the Eurobond and mortgage-backed securities market by brokers and dealers in the 1970s and 1980s. The US Federal Reserve recognized this as a potential market by allowing rule changes that enabled dealers to perform similar exercises with government bonds. The technique involved is known as 'stripping', and the securities created in STRIPS exercises are zero-coupon bonds. STRIPS stands for 'Separate Trading of Registered Interest and Principal of Securities'. The way strips work in the UK market is described in brief in the sidebar.

The UK tax treatment of zeros is not entirely straightforward. The main reason is that the UK Treasury doesn't take lightly the prospect of losing the tax revenue from gilt-edge interest income caused by the creation of strips, which effectively converts income into capital growth. The result has been that gilt strips do fall within the CGT regime.

The way this works is as follows. Holders generate a capital gains tax liability as normal if they sell within a year, and are deemed to have 'bed and breakfasted' the gilt if they hold it from one year to the next. How this works is no real mystery. The Revenue simply deems that the holder sells the stock at the closing price on 5 April and repurchases the same security on 6 April. From one tax year to the next, the cost of the stock for CGT purchases is therefore the book cost of the stock at the opening price on 6 April.

Strips could in theory be most attractive for low or non-taxpaying private investors. Paradoxically, of course, these are precisely the investors who have a pressing need for current income. However, strips may have appeal for frugal standard rate taxpayers with low overheads and sizeable capital. There is an obvious section of the population that falls into this

S I D E B A R

How zeros are created

A conventional gilt-edge stock – provided it falls within the list of 'strippable' gilts' – is bought in the market (or at issue) by a market maker or investment bank. The number of coupons remaining to maturity and their value are calculated and stripped into the same number of separate securities with a nominal value equating to the coupon.

The principal payment becomes a further zero-coupon stock with a much higher nominal value. Hence £1 million of a 10-year government bond with a 5% coupon paid semi-annually acquired by a market maker at par can be stripped into 21 separate securities.

There will be 20 zeros of differing maturities based around the coupon. One of these will each mature at six-monthly intervals from the next interest payment date to the redemption date. Each will have a redemption value of £25,000. This is the amount paid on the nominal value of £1m at each successive interest half-yearly interest payment date.

The final zero-coupon security (based on the £1m principal) has a nominal value of £1m and a maturity date that corresponds to the redemption date of the original stock.

The issue value of each separate zero depends on its length of time to maturity. It is calculated by taking the appropriate risk-free yield as a discount rate and using the discount technique described in Chapter 2, working out the notional present value accordingly.

If interest rate expectations change the value of all zeros – and particularly a longer maturity one – will be affected. If rates are expected to rise, values will fall. If the reverse, other things being equal, their values will rise.

Most investors in zero-coupon bonds are pension funds. Zero-coupon securities exist in other forms, such as zero dividend preference shares issued by split capital investment trusts. These tend to be used more actively by private investors.

category. These are doting grandparents who want to provide for their grandchildren's education. In other words, strips work well for those with a specific savings target several years hence.

The Treasury's Debt Management Office decides which gilts are strippable at the time of issue. The stocks listed in Table 6.5 are those currently designated as strippable.

Strippable stocks are, as might be expected, those which are the most liquid – that is, those which have the highest nominal amount currently outstanding. The least liquid is the 6.5% of 2003 (£2000m in issue) and the most liquid the 8% of 2021 (£16,500m issue).

There are no undated stocks in the list, because clearly for the discounting principle to work, the stock must have a finite life. Finally, there is gap in the strippable stocks list between maturity dates in 2007 and 2015.

Table 6.5 Gilt-edge ticker codes – strippable stocks

Coupon	Maturity	Code
7.0	7.6.02	TR2
6.5	12.7.03	T6H3
8.5	7.12.05	TR05
7.5	7.12.06	TR6
7.25	7.12.07	T07
8.0	7.12.15	TY8
8.0	7.6.21	TR21
6.0	7.12.28	TR28
4.25	7.6.32	TR32

Convertibles

Convertible bonds (and their close cousins, exchangeable bonds) are invariably corporate bonds. They are a hybrid. Two types of security are combined: a straight bond with a relatively low coupon on the one hand, and an option to buy the underlying shares at a specific fixed price after a certain date on the other. My book *Traded Options – A Private Investors' Guide* (Financial Times Prentice Hall 2001) explains how options work in detail.

Convertible bonds are a hybrid.

An option confers the right to buy (a call option) or sell (a put option) a specific number of shares at a fixed exercise (or strike) price for a period of time in the future, after which time the option will expire worthless or be converted into the underlying shares it represents.

A call option is said to be in-the-money if the price of the underlying shares is above the strike price. Conversely, a call option is out-of-the-money if the share price of the underlying is less than the share price.

When issued, the embedded option in a convertible normally does not kick in (i.e. the bond does not become convertible) until some years after the issue is made. Nonetheless the conversion facility in the bond, as represented by the embedded option, can be valued very precisely for any given value of the underlying shares (Table 6.6).

It follows that valuing convertibles can be done by valuing the bond component as a straight bond on the normal redemption yield basis. This means using a comparable government bond as a reference point, but applying an appropriate additional spread over and above the government bond to reflect any additional risk (however small that might be) inherent in a corporate bond.

The embedded option can also be valued according to the normal formula used for valuing options. The important variables here are the volatility of the underlying shares, the share price level at which the option can be exercised, the current price of the shares, and the length of time until the option expires.

The yield-based value of the bond component and the value of the option feature can then be added together to arrive at a 'fair value' for the convertible, and this value compared with the market price.

Exchangeable bonds are convertibles where the embedded option allows the holder to convert into the shares of a company other than the issuer. Here it is even more important that the two components are separately valued: the bond component in part by reflecting on the quality

Table 6.6 Valuing convertible components

Value by reference to	
Bond	Option
Yield on benchmark	Price of underlying shares versus exercise price
Credit quality of issuer	Time to expiry of conversion feature
Interest rate prospects	Volatility of underlying shares

of the issuer; the option component by reflecting on the prospects (favourable or otherwise) for the likely medium-term course of share price of the company whose shares represent the 'underlying' for the option.

In short, a judgement needs to be made about the prospects for the underlying company's share price, and of the equity market as a whole. We will give some concrete examples of how convertibles can be valued in Chapter 8, but suffice to say that bonds are often bought by investors as an each-way bet during bear markets. This is because they combine the relative safety of a bond, with modest participation (through the embedded option feature) in any upward movement in the underlying share.

Exchangeable bonds are less common, but examples have cropped up recently. In the recent flotation of Orange by France Telecom, bonds were issued by France Telecom that were convertible, or rather exchangeable, into Orange shares. Much more on this – including some worked examples – in Chapter 8.

Irredeemables

Irredeemable stocks – sometimes in other markets called 'perpetual' stocks or perpetuities – are government bonds that pay a semi-annual coupon but have no repayment date. As such they have infinite duration and are particularly sensitive to changes in expectation about interest rates.

The two classic irredeemable stocks in the gilt-edge market are $2\frac{1}{2}$% Consols (ticker symbol CN2H) and War Loan, a stock with a $3\frac{1}{2}$% coupon (ticker symbol WAR). These issues respectively have £275m and £1909m nominal of stock in issue. There is also a slightly larger Consol (or Consolidated stock) in issue with a 4% coupon. The ticker symbol for 4% Consols is CN4. There is also $2\frac{1}{2}$% Treasury stock with £474m in issue (ticker symbol T2H), which was redeemable at the government's option at any time after 1975 and so far has not been (Table 6.7).

The name of one of these stocks reflects the use to which it was originally put. War Loan was used to help finance World War I. Imagine

Table 6.7 Ticker codes for irredeemable stocks

Stock	Coupon	Ticker
Consols	2.5	CN2H
Consols	4.0	CN4
War Loan	3.5	WAR
Treasury	2.5	T2H

the amount in issue converted back to 1914 pounds and you get some idea of the original size of the stock in real terms. Paradoxically, there is speculation of occasional offers to redeem irredeemable stocks, although one suspects that War Loan in particular is so much a market icon that it is unlikely ever to meet its maker.

It is important to stress, however, that these stocks are far from being risk free. Since there is no guarantee that the principal amount invested will ever be repaid, market perceptions about interest rates are virtually the only factor that govern the price. On a recent occasion in March 2001 when rate cuts were deemed less likely and the stock market fell by 2% in a single day, the $2^1/2\%$ Treasury stock fell by 1%, as did War Loan. The other two active stocks did not change, but this reflects extreme illiquidity as much as anything.

If interest rates are cut further, should the prices of undated stocks not rise? It might seem logical to suppose so, but it isn't necessarily likely to happen. The reason is as follows. As noted in Chapter 3, the UK yield curve, one of the prime determinants of the way the gilt-edge market moves, is currently inverted. This means that yields at the long-dated end of the curve are below those of short-dated stocks. In part this has been due, as explained earlier, to the penchant of pension funds to invest in long-dated gilts to meet the need to finance future liabilities for pensions. Pension fund demand has driven up the price and therefore depressed the yields of these securities.

Irredeemable stocks usually take their cue from the longest dated redeemable stock, currently the Treasury $4^3/4\%$ 2032. If short-term interest rates fall, however, all that is likely to happen (indeed may have happened by the publication of this book) is that the yield curve will pivot around the long and undated end. Interest rates will likely stimulate economic growth and so increase the chances of UK inflation rising, thus depressing the attractiveness of irredeemable stocks.

Unless the government redeems these stocks, the only conceivable reason for buying now would be if the UK were to enter a 30-year period when inflation was below the running yield on a long-dated, index-linked bond. These are currently around 2.267%. Short of redemption, the odds on the UK experiencing inflation below 2.267% continuously for 30 years are so remote as to be infinitesimal. Even if it were to be the case, the 4.37% running yield on the current 'long bond' maturing in 2032 would be better value.

Those seeking better value among irredeemable stocks are better advised to concentrate on so-called PIBS (Perpetual Interest Bearing Securities). These are stocks issued by banks, building societies and companies.

Callable and puttable bonds

Little used in the UK corporate bond market, these are similar to convertibles in the sense that they are hybrids of a straight bond and an embedded option.

In the case of a callable bond, the issuer has the option to redeem at a specific price and on a specific date if it is in its interest to do so. This means the bond has to have a higher coupon to compensate the holder for the risk the bond will be redeemed early by the issuer exercising the embedded call option.

In the case of a puttable bond, the holder has the right to sell the bonds back to the issuer at a specific price and on a specific date, if it is in his or her interest to do so. This means the bond has a lower coupon to compensate the issuer for the risk that the bond will be redeemed early by the holder exercising the embedded put option.

In both cases and as with convertibles, the two components of the bonds can be separately valued and then combined to arrive at a fair value. This can then be compared with the market price to work out whether or not the bond is cheap.

Unlike convertibles, however, the option relates to the bond itself, not the underlying equity, which means that a buyer has to judge the likely trend in interest rates. Falls (or expected falls) in interest rates make the callable bond more likely to be called by the issuer, since it will be able to repay the bond and refinance at lower rates.

Rising interest rates (or expectations that rates will rise) hand the initiative to the investor to sell back the bonds to the issuer by exercising the put option. The investor can then take advantage of higher returns available elsewhere.

While not entirely risk free (although bank PIBS are probably as near to it as makes no difference), they carry a more generous coupon than undated gilts and can be bought and sold in the market. At the time of writing yields on PIBS ranged from 7.2% to 7.5%.

Other

There is a range of other securities that fall into the category of oddball bonds. These include: extendibles and retractables; sinking fund bonds; inverse floaters.

Extendibles and retractables

These are bonds issued by some governments and companies that have maturity dates which can be lengthened or shortened at specific times at the issuer's discretion.

Sinking fund bonds

These are corporate bonds with a fixed coupon where, rather than repay the principal amount invested, a percentage of it is repaid with each interest payment.

Inverse floaters

These are like floating rate notes (see earlier in this chapter) but the coupon paid varies inversely with the reference rate (such as LIBOR) with the rate having a cap rather than a floor. The first of these was the Student Loan Marketing Association (Sallie Mae) inverse floater in the USA, where the coupon rate was set at 17.2% minus six months LIBOR.

These instruments are in the main strictly for professionals only, but a useful way of playing an expected downward movement in rates from what is expected to be an historically high level. Even so-called professional investors make mistakes. To underscore the potential risk involved in these instruments, it is perhaps worth noting that it was a product deriving from an inverse floater which was responsible for the bankruptcy of Orange County in California in the mid-1990s.

Inverse floaters, PIBS, convertibles, extendibles, retractables, callables and puttables are generally the preserve of the Eurobond and corporate bond markets and will be covered in more detail (along with straight bonds in these categories) in the next two chapters.

IN BRIEF

- There are a number of variations on the bond theme. Most of these have one or more of the essential elements of a bond either modified or absent.

- Index-linked bonds adjust the principal and interest payments to allow for changes in the RPI. They provide a modest inflation proofed return.

- Floating rate notes have a coupon payment that changes based on a reference rate of interest. They are frequently used as a tax-efficient alternative to a cash payment in a takeover.

- Zero-coupon bonds are created via a process known as stripping being applied to conventional government bonds. Zeros have no coupon, but are priced at a deep discount to their redemption value. They are attractive for those with specific long-term savings targets to meet.

- Irredeemable bonds have a fixed coupon but no maturity date.

- Convertible and exchange bonds are conventional bonds with the addition of an inbuilt option to convert into underlying ordinary shares. The bond component and the option component can be valued separately to work out if the bond is cheap.

chapter seven

Eurobonds

The usual definition of a Eurobond is that it is a bond denominated in any currency other than that of the issuer. Eurobonds are sold to investors outside the country where the issuer has its legal home. The typical issuers of bonds like this are diverse. Major multinationals and their subsidiaries, sovereign governments, local authorities, banks and supranational organizations such as the World Bank or IMF all issue Eurobonds. Issuers use bonds like this for a variety of purposes. These include short-term working capital, project finance and permanent capital funding.

> The usual definition of a Eurobond is that it is a bond denominated in any currency other than that of the issuer.

Eurobonds come in the familiar 'straight' format with a coupon and a maturity date, but also in all other shapes and sizes. Many of these reflect the exotic structures described in the previous chapter.

Short history of the Eurobond market

These days the Eurobond market is a less exciting place than it once was. One reason is that the interplay between the currencies of countries making up the Euro-zone is no longer present.

UK and US companies typically issue bonds denominated in Euros and Yen. Euro-zone entities issue in Euro Sterling, Euro Yen and Eurodollars. There have been some issues, especially from development agencies, in the currencies of emerging markets (see below).

While all this might seem reasonably mundane, the market has had a colourful history. The market existed in a small way for many decades, but it first came to prominence rather by accident. This was the result of inept measures initiated by President Kennedy in 1963. Kennedy's measure was called the interest equalization tax (IET). It was a form of reverse globalization of the capital markets. The tax made it more expensive for non-US companies to raise money in the USA by making it more costly for US residents to hold foreign stocks and bonds. In effect, US residents faced a 15% sales tax if they bought investments like this. The USA eventually abolished the tax in 1974, but the Eurobond market's strong growth in the intervening years stemmed directly from it.

The first bond to benefit from the imposition of IET was issued to finance Italian autostradas, announced just before the IET was imposed. In 1965 Germany also got in on the act. It imposed a 25% withholding tax on coupon payments paid to non-residents holding German government bonds and those of domestic companies and banks. The purpose was the reverse of the US move: it was to deflect capital inflows. Bonds issued in Deutschemarks outside Germany were exempt. This gave a further boost to the Euro markets.

In 1965, President Johnson promoted further legislation to limit capital outflows from the USA. This limited the amounts that US banks could lend to overseas companies and the extent to which US companies could raise funds at home to invest overseas. The result was that foreign branches and subsidiaries of US banks built up unused dollar deposits offshore.

Prior to all this there had been an international bond market of sorts, but the upshot of all these measures was to enlarge the pool of Euro-currencies, particularly Eurodollars and Euro marks. Eurocurrencies are currencies deposited in banks outside their country of origin and used to settle international transactions.

The capital restrictions also provided the impetus for a variety of international organizations to tap into this pool more than they had before. They saw it as way of obtaining finance cheaper than in their home market. Large bond issues in Eurocurrencies were the result. This brought about the explosive growth of the Eurobond market. It was largely based in London. Eurobonds had been issued and traded before, but were seen as something of a backwater. For this reason, old-style London brokers at the time dismissed the Eurobond market as an oddity. Even after it developed into a large market, they tended to decry it as a 'commodity' business and were not keen to participate. They preferred their own brand of more genteel 'bespoke' corporate finance.

Nonetheless some of the more prominent pioneers of the Eurobond market were key players in the London broking scene. Among them was Siegmund Warburg, the legendary founder of SG Warburg (now Warburg Dillon Reed and part of UBS). Another firm deeply involved in the market from the start was Strauss Turnbull, led by the equally seminal figure of Julius Strauss. The role both played in the Euromarkets made them very much the exception to their broking peers.

The gap that could have been filled by more imaginative UK brokers did not remain open for long. The inventive minds in the securities offshoots of European banks and the offshore offices of US investment banks saw this as a highly lucrative business, with vast fee-earning potential. They grabbed at the opportunity quickly. As distinct from staid government bond markets, Eurobonds allowed investment bank rocket scientists to create complex new structures to satisfy the demands of their clients for cheap finance.

> Eurobonds allowed investment bank rocket scientists to create complex new structures to satisfy the demands of their clients for cheap finance.

Also attractive to issuers was the fact that investment banks could place bonds with a broad spread of investors. Among these were affluent private investors, who would typically buy the bonds at issue, hold to maturity and essentially be passive holders. Many innovations came along to tempt these investors. Convertibles, exchangeables, callable and puttable bonds, zero-coupon bonds, FRNs and all the other paraphernalia of the Eurobond market grew up. Many were first developed specifically for the Eurobond market, or adapted from structures previously devised in the USA (Table 7.1).

To say that many investors in Eurobonds are private is an understatement. A key characteristic of Eurobonds is that these bearer bonds allowed investors to remain anonymous. At times this led to the assumption that some possibly had good reason to remain so (and not just from a tax avoidance standpoint). Bearer bonds are unregistered and simply deemed the property of the person who presents them.

The second key development was the establishment, through organizations like Euroclear and Cedel (the latter now called Clearstream), of an efficient mechanism for settling trades in Eurobonds. Euroclear was an offshoot of Morgan Guaranty, a key player in the Eurobond market. Morgan spread ownership of Euroclear among its customers, mainly leading European banks.

The Eurobond market has advantages for all who participate in it, but

Table 7.1 Five key characteristics of Eurobonds

1.	Bearer (therefore anonymous)
2.	Illiquid trading
3.	Pricing not transparent
4.	Big name issuers
5.	Variety of structures

these do not come without risks attached. In particular, because investors hold them for long periods, once issued many bonds are infrequently traded. Consequently, investors find it hard to know – if they want to buy or sell – whether or not the market price is a fair one. The bid-offer spread may also be wider than is the case with government bonds. ISMA estimates, for example, that there may be as many as 40,000 bonds outstanding, of which only 500 or so are traded actively at any one time.

S I D E B A R

A note on Eurobond realpolitik

By their nature, Eurobonds appeal to affluent individuals residing in continental Europe. One reason is that the bonds are portable, so-called 'bearer', bonds – not specifically registered to an identifiable holder. Typical holders are wealthy Belgian, Dutch, German, French and Swiss private investors, and some UK-based corporate bond funds. Market wags say that the typical Eurobond investor is an affluent Belgian dentist. Because there are no border controls within the Schengen group, these investors have easy access by car to continental tax havens, where bonds can be lodged and interest collected away from prying eyes.

At the behest of the German government, the European Commission recently proposed to apply EU-wide a 20% withholding tax on income derived from Eurobonds. One feature of the proposal was that banks collecting the interest on behalf of bondholders would be compelled to provide this information to the relevant tax authority. This clearly had implications for banking secrecy laws in tax havens, as well as being administratively complex.

The British government, however, feared that the threat of a withholding tax would kill off issue activity in what has long been one of the City's biggest fee-earning businesses.

Treasury mandarins working in Brussels have been insisting that a reciprocal information exchange between tax authorities is the only practical way to handle this without compromising banking secrecy rules in some member states. This approach has been adopted in principle. To be implemented, however, each member state's tax authority has to agree to exchange information with every other one – an impossible task. This solution, worthy of Sir Humphrey himself, kills off any thoughts that the withholding tax can be imposed in practice.

There are data and comment on some recent bond issues later in the chapter. Unlike today's issues, some of the early bond issues were minute. A $10m issue was not unknown. Today the figures are usually in the $100–500m range and some are much larger. 'Jumbo' issues of $5bn for major issuers and well-known bankable names are commonplace.

Any history of the Eurobond market would not be complete without some mention of the Association of International Bond Dealers (AIBD), set up in 1969 to act as a trade association for the market. The AIBD's first annual meeting was held in the rather staid setting of the Intercontinental Hotel in Geneva. But as the market boomed, the AGMs of AIBD became ever-larger events in increasingly exotic locations. They inevitably produced a steady diet of rumours about the eccentric late night behaviour of certain members of the Eurobond community who had entertained well, if not wisely. Today the AIBD is now ISMA, the International Securities Market Association. It has become, as have all such entities, a more sober, responsible and arguably less freewheeling organization than its predecessor.

How Eurobond underwriting works

How does Eurobond underwriting work? Take a typical issue. It is a straight bond denominated in dollars and issued by a French corporation – a classic Eurodollar issue. The issuer issues the bonds in the first instance to a group of large investment banks. They function as a syndicate to

SIDEBAR

Tombstones

Lead manager and syndicate roles are coveted positions and magazines draw up league tables of the banks taking these roles. Brokers and banks advertise their league table standings and often issue self-congratulatory advertisements each year listing the clients in whose bond financings they have played a role, however minor.

Each bond issue usually has its own 'tombstone', an advertisement that states who the lead manager and syndicate members were. In one of the bizarre rituals of the Eurobond market, tombstones are usually also produced encased in small acetate blocks and distributed to syndicate members as souvenirs.

market the bonds to investors. One bank (sometimes two) acts as a lead (or co-lead) manager, overseeing the whole process. The syndicate might comprise one or two (or more, depending on the banking structure of the country concerned) smaller banks and brokers in each of the markets outside the issuer's home market.

In this example, this would mean any country in the world other than France. In the case of a bond from a French issuer, the natural home for the bonds would be elsewhere in Europe. It is here that the appetite for these bonds will probably be greatest. Swiss banks and specialist UK brokers might also be involved.

The syndicate buys the bonds from the issue managers at a slight discount to the underwriting price and bonds are then marketed to investors at their face (or 'par') value or slightly below.

The lead manager sets the price to balance supply and demand for the bonds, while leaving a cut for the issue managers themselves. If the bond is popular, it is likely that the lead managers will try and hog the issue. The degree of hogging permitted depends on the parameters set by the issuer, who may want to see the issue spread across a broad range of investors in different countries. In a case of blatant hogging by the lead manager or managers, the syndicate banks and brokers will have little to show for their efforts in marketing the issue.

SIDEBAR

How syndicates work in practice

Lead managers get it wrong too, which can lead to the bond being overpriced and everyone suffering. I was involved personally in a Eurobond issue during my career working for a UK investment bank. I spent time marketing an issue to clients and organized a roadshow to an exotic location for potential investors in the bond from across Europe. In this instance, our allocation of bonds was cut at the last minute. The lead manager's explanation when we protested: 'I've changed my mind.'

We then compounded the error by taking the allocation of the bond – several million pounds worth – onto the firm's books. It immediately went to a two-point discount on our purchase price, producing an instant loss of around £200,000. Red faces all round.

Eurobond pricing

Issue managers price Eurobonds by reference either to US Treasuries or the Euro-zone government bond market yield curve. They make an appropriate adjustment for the perceived credit quality of the issuer. The issue is sold to investors on the basis of a yield (calculated on the offer price) that equates to the benchmark yield plus the appropriate number of basis points above.

Take, for *example*, an issue of a EUR 500m 5% 15-year bond. The Euro-zone government bond yield curve suggests the appropriate benchmark yield for a 15-year bond is 4.7%. The credit quality of the issuer, a major subsidiary of a Dow Jones Industrial Average company, suggests that the spread over the benchmark should be 80 basis points (i.e. 0.8%).

The lead manager would therefore set the issue's price so as to yield 5.5% to a buyer. The syndicate would buy bonds from the lead manager at a discount representing say 50% of the spread and market them to investors. In this case, the proceeds to this hypothetical issuer would be 95.2% of face value, or EUR475m. The fees on the issue would be split 50/50 between the lead manager and all the banks in the syndicate. (The numbers in this example are from an actual recent issue.)

Little wonder then, that investment banks fight like dogs for lead manager places and are very sensitive to the way the league tables are calculated. A major row erupted in 2000 when the best-known publisher of the league tables proposed a change to the way lead managers were credited in the table (Table 7.2). Energetic lobbying by the leading investment banks resulted in the proposal being quietly dropped and status quo restored. A cynic might speculate that the lobbying included threats to pull the massive advertising revenue generated by 'tombstone' advertising. Sadly there is no concrete way of verifying that such threats were made.

Table 7.2 Eurobond pricing – who gets what

	%
Investor pays	100
Bond mid-price	99.5
Syndicate members pay	99
Lead manager pays	98
Fees for issue managers	0.8
Issuer receives	97.2

For more on credit quality – which applies across all segments of the bond market – see the next chapter on corporate bonds. This includes a detailed examination of the way credit rating agencies make their decisions. Credit quality is one of the main determinants of a bond's

SIDEBAR

The role of the swap curve

Many Eurobond issues, especially those denominated in currencies other than the dollar, have prices that are set by reference to the swap curve. Interest rate swaps enable financial institutions and/or companies to trade differing views about whether rates will fall or rise.

A company might prefer to issue a floating rate obligation if it thought rates were falling. But market conditions or the precise timing of its cash flow requirements, which dictate the timing of a bond issue, mean it could only issue a fixed rate bond. At the same time, a financial institution might on the contrary believe that rates were likely to stay the same or rise over the long term, in which case it would prefer to borrow on the basis of a fixed rate.

The two institutions can exchange these obligations via the medium of the swaps market. The institution gets its fixed rate borrowing while the corporation picks up the floating rate liability. Swaps are actively traded for many issues of different quality. They are measured on a yield basis.

Deducting the respective spreads over the benchmark from the implied yields at which these swaps are dealt results in the swap yield curve (or swap curve). Because of the volume of trade in the swaps market, and the infinite variety of issues traded, the swap curve – though a synthetic creation – is probably the purest expression of a yield curve. It is therefore a better yardstick on which to base the pricing of Eurobonds of disparate quality.

Swap curve information is hard to come by for private investors. The swaps market is exclusively between corporate treasury departments and investment banks. Without professional terminals such as those from financial information providers such as Bloomberg, investors have no way of discovering the information at first hand. The European issue of the *Wall Street Journal* occasionally publishes statistics and a graph of the Euro-zone swap curve.

value. How bonds like this are valued therefore depends on several important factors, of which credit quality is just one:

■ coupon

■ precise maturity date

■ price to a buyer at issue

■ benchmark yield

■ perceived credit quality of issuer

■ outlook for underlying securities (convertibles)

■ outlook for currency of issue.

For straight bonds in particular, the credit rating and perceived credit quality of the issuer is probably the single most important determinant of whether an issue will do well. At the time an issue is made, all other variables are fixed. Investors therefore have to judge whether or not the yield compensates adequately for any perceived credit risk. Credit risk must be examined dispassionately. It does not, as some investors assume, simply equate a company's reputation and how well or otherwise it is known.

Eurobonds and emerging markets – a digression

Companies use Eurobonds for mundane financings and refinancings, whether through straight bonds, FRNs or commercial paper (the latter is an ultra-short-term money market instrument). Supranational organizations and occasionally multinational companies occasionally (sometimes often) tap the Eurobond market for funds. Supranationals are entities such as the World Bank, its offshoot the International Finance Corporation (IFC), the European Bank for Reconstruction & Development (EBRD) and the Inter-American Development Bank (IDB). All of these institutions provide financing either for so-called transition economies or for other developing countries. From time to time they use bond issues as a way of encouraging the development of capital markets and foreign investment interest in these economies (Table 7.3).

In the past they have issued bonds in Czech koruna, South Korean won, Argentine pesos, Polish zlotys, South African rand and many other currencies. Lest one get the idea that these entities are behaving in any way altruistically by doing this, it's worth noting that a supranational will swap the proceeds of the issue instantly into US dollars. It often regards the whole exercise as a way of getting its hands on cut-price funding. For the countries themselves, bond issues like this are an important development.

Table 7.3 Emerging market Eurobonds – who are the issuers?

Typical issuers	Typical currencies
World Bank	South African rand
IFC	South Korean won
IDB	Czech koruna
EBRD	Israeli shekel
Large corporates	Turkish lira

This is particularly true if their domestic government bond market is small and illiquid, which is often the case.

Despite devaluations and political uncertainty, Eurobond issues in exotic currencies – with a top drawer issuer involved – look set to be a permanent, if intermittent, part of the investment scene. Though important, they can be a mixed blessing for the governments concerned. While they signal that capital markets are developing in the country, the worry is that as these markets develop they may also trigger currency volatility. One reason cited by many market players for their earlier popularity was the coming of the Euro and the need for investors (and of course syndicate managers) to broaden the portfolio of currencies they traded in.

These moves are partly explained by the need for basic diversification. But, more to the point perhaps, investors are also trying to identify and take advantage of the next 'convergence play'. Convergence is where a country comes to be seen as a likely member of the international community, or a specific member of an entity like the EU, and yields on its bonds move towards the much lower ones ruling in the wider sphere.

The other motive is simply that bond issues from supranationals and top-tier corporates offer both a solid 'name' but a substantial pick-up in yield for the investor. While they run currency risk, investors can benefit later if economic trends suggest that a permanent move towards a lower yield basis is warranted by the country's economic performance.

That was the theory. While not disproving it entirely, Russian bond defaults in 1998, the more recent devaluation of the Turkish lira and uncertainty in the Middle East have tested investors' patience to the limit. At the very least, events like this prove the risks are real ones. Issues in the currencies of Russia, Turkey and Israel, as well as those of Korea and Thailand, were all the rage at one time. Higher than normal yields were supposed to compensate for the risks involved, but in many instances they didn't.

Investors have to make a judgement about the risks involved. Possibilities of EU membership are seen as a good guide. Countries whose economies are closer to the western-style norm and where full currency convertibility may be round the corner are likely to be better risks. Convertibility is seen as moving the market into the mainstream, and therefore a more appropriate one for the private investor to participate in (Table 7.4).

At one time, Greek drachma bonds were popular, prompted by thoughts that the currency could enter the Euro in the second wave, and the consequent positioning of bond issues in drachmae from strong international credits as convergence plays. Indeed, drachmae issues have epitomized the convergence argument for investing in emerging paper. Generally the exercise has been a success.

Turkish lire issues were also much in evidence at the same time. Here the outcome has been different. Spectacular yields on these bonds reflected higher internal inflation and greater certainty of currency depreciation. What investors were looking for here, though, was a stable or improving economic situation and a substantial pick-up in yield versus Bunds or US Treasuries. But such gains do not come without currency risk attached, as the subsequent Turkish devaluation demonstrated.

Are emerging market Eurobonds here to stay? Probably, since they offer advantages for issuers, for issue managers, and potentially for investors – if they pick the right issue and can live with currency volatility. For governments contemplating opening up their economies to international investors, the advantages may be less obvious, if indeed they exist at all.

> **Are emerging market Eurobonds here to stay?**

Policy makers in these countries can see the advantages of having western-style capital markets on the one hand, but they fret about the volatile flows of money they bring with them on the other. Some, however, believe that bonds like these are to be encouraged. The argument is that they serve a useful function if they allow market infrastructure to be developed. The extreme view is that capital markets may sometimes need to be created to offset the deficiencies in the capabilities of the domestic banking system.

Table 7.4 Emerging market Eurobonds – what are the issues?

For investors	For governments
Currency risk	Development of capital markets
Chances of convergences	International exposure
Liquidity	Risk of 'hot money'
Type of bond	Strength of banking system
Volatility	Political stability

One thing that the Asian crisis may have taught is that emerging countries can't necessarily rely on your banking system. If the banking system isn't robust, then developing capital markets becomes a priority. While emerging market debt issues have at times been popular with investors and issuers, the potential volatility of the flows of money created remains the biggest downside for governments. They want to ensure relative currency stability. A ballooning Eurocurrency debt market sets up the conditions where any perceived shortcomings in economic performance, or any hints of political instability, can upset the currency apple-cart.

The problem for governments is that when Eurobonds are launched in a country's own currency it gives foreign investors claims over that economy. Cynics say, and the Turkish example may bear this out, that a booming local currency Euro-debt market can be almost an early warning indicator of trouble. For these reasons some countries have adopted an alternative method of bringing their country's merits to the attention of international investors. They have done this by launching bonds backed by their governments but in foreign currencies. Yields are higher than benchmark government bonds. The bonds are not immune from default, but investors avoid undue currency risk. Romania, Croatia, Argentina and Turkey have been among the countries to tap the market in this way in 2001.

Types of Eurobond

This section recaps in brief the characteristics of several common types of bond and gives concrete examples of Eurobond issues taking these forms. These are:

- straight bonds
- floating rate notes
- zero-coupon bonds
- convertible bonds
- callable and puttable bonds.

Straight bonds

As explained early on in the book, straight bonds have a fixed annual coupon, usually paid once or twice yearly, and single maturity date when all of the principal amount is repaid.

Example: Telecom Italia issued a bond like this in April 2001. This EUR6bn issue was mounted in several currency tranches. The largest of these, at EUR3bn, was a straight bond carrying a coupon of 6.125%. The price was 99.937%, and the bond had a maturity of 20 April 2006. Telecom Italia was rated a single A borrower. At around the same time France Telecom, rated BBB, issued £600m of bonds with a 7.5% coupon and a maturity of March 2011.

The distinction between other bonds and their 'straight' cousins is that, in contrast to 'straight' bonds, the variants usually have one or more of the key bond components either absent or adjusted, or else have additional features.

Floating rate notes

These have a coupon that floats up or down by reference to a benchmark or reference rate. A normal floater is issued with a coupon based on a reference rate (usually LIBOR or EURIBOR) plus a fixed number of basis points. It has a capped rate. An inverse floater has a coupon fixed by reference to a fixed rate minus the yield on three-month LIBOR (or EURIBOR). It has a floor rate.

Example: One recent example of a floater was an issue from the Alstom subsidiary Cruise Ship Finance. This was part of regular series of issues to finance the building of new cruise ships for RCL. This issue of EUR324m had a one-year maturity. The issue price implied a yield of EURIBOR plus 170 basis points. Investors in bonds like this are repaid when the ship is delivered. The issuer had a BBB credit rating.

Zero-coupon bonds

With zero-coupon bonds, there is no coupon. Investors get their return from the movement in the price towards par as the bond approaches its maturity date.

Example: An example of a recent zero-coupon issue was one from the Nordic Investment Bank. This EUR350m issue (the issue's size was increased from EUR250m) had a maturity date in April 2016. The price of 45.95, implied a yield to maturity of 5.25%.

Extendibles and retractables

These have a fixed coupon but a variable maturity date, usually at the issuer's option. Callable and puttable bonds are used in the UK corporate bond market and the Eurobond market. These are similar to convertibles in the sense that they are hybrids of a straight bond and an embedded option.

Callable bonds

In the case of a callable bond, the issuer has the option to redeem at a specific price and on a specific date if it is in its interest to do so. This means the bond has to have a higher coupon to compensate the holder for the risk the bond will be redeemed early by the issuer exercising the embedded call option.

Puttable bonds

In the case of a puttable bond, the holder has the right to sell the bonds back to the issuer at a specific price and on a specific date, if it is in his or her interest to do so. This means the bond has a lower coupon to compensate the issuer for the risk that the bond will be redeemed early by the holder exercising the embedded put option.

Convertible bonds

Convertible bonds are effectively 'straight' bonds with options to switch into a fixed number of shares in the issuer at a predetermined price. Exchangeables are like convertibles, but the option is to switch into the shares of a company other than the issuer. Investors can value the embedded option (an out-of-the-money call option) separately using a conventional option-pricing model.

Example: One recent big exchangeable bond issue was a $2.66bn from Hutchison Whampoa (an A-rated borrower). This had a coupon of 2.5% and a three-year maturity. It was exchangeable into shares of Vodafone with the conversion premium 28% above the then ruling price of Vodafone's shares.

Example: About the same size was the EUR3.1bn exchangeable bond issued by France Telecom at the time of the Orange share issue. This bond had a maturity of two years and a conversion premium of 27% over the issue price of Orange shares.

It is worth pointing out that each of these types is common to most bond markets, whether government or corporate. Each type has its particular spin in the terms and conditions such bonds work under, and their tax treatment may also differ.

High-yield bonds

High-yield (or so-called 'junk') bond issues are now a recognized part of the Eurobond scene. 'Junk' denotes issues deemed to be 'below investment grade' by rating agencies. This is anything with a credit rating below BBB.

Example: A recent example of high-yield issue was one from the Swedish refinery Preem Holdings AB. It issued EUR250m of bonds with a 10.625% coupon maturing in April 2011. This issue had a yield of 590 basis points over the yield on the 10-year Bund issue.

Accessibility of Eurobonds to the private investor

For the broad mass of private investors in the UK, direct investment in Eurobonds is unlikely. Brokers and banks do sell Eurobonds to some high net worth individuals. Market professionals generally advise, however, that private investors take advice before investing and, equally importantly, make sure as far as possible that their broker has access to experts in the field.

> For the broad mass of private investors in the UK, direct investment in Eurobonds is unlikely.

Clients of larger brokers may have access to new Eurobond issues if their broker is part of the syndicate or an issue manager. Such offers need to be scrutinized carefully. In cases like this, brokers sometimes sell bonds to 'retail' investors when the professionals have given them a lukewarm reception.

Investors should study credit quality. Although there is an understandable tendency for investors to opt for bonds from names they know, astute investors can profit from this by doing the opposite. Bargains can crop up because unfamiliar names may in fact have better credit quality, or even a government guarantee. This is particularly true of bonds issued by some lesser known German banks.

> Investors should study credit quality.

Many professionals suggest confining investment in Eurobonds generally to banks. The simple reason is that banks live or die by maintaining a solid credit rating. This is because their cost of borrowing is one of their main operating costs, and maintaining a good credit rating is one way of minimizing this.

This contrasts with companies, where ill-judged acquisitions can result in a sharp deterioration in credit ratings. If so, it means that investors in earlier bond issues will suffer deterioration in price as yields increase to reflect the lowered credit rating. This is called 'event risk'.

The risks and specialized nature of the market suggest that many investors should invest in Eurobonds through the medium of corporate bond funds rather than directly. We cover funds like this in detail in Chapter 10.

Basic information on Eurobonds is sparse. ISMA publishes a weekly guide to about 7500 issues, but these guides cost £40 apiece. The guides give details of the issues including minimum investment size, indicative price, yield, duration, credit rating and a number of other important statistics. ISMA (www.isma.org) is in the process of enabling some of this information for the web. It will be available to investors in due course, probably via a subscription service. There is some market data at Reuters Credit (http://credit.reuters.com), also mainly on a subscription basis. The websites of investment banks also offer some information on Eurobonds, but much of it is in client-only areas.

IN BRIEF

- Eurobonds are bonds issued in currencies other than those of the issuer's domicile.

- The Eurobond market has a long history. Issue activity is dominated by major investment banks, which manage and underwrite large numbers of issues each year.

- Eurobonds are popular with continental investors, partly because of their portability and tax efficiency.

- Issues take place in a wide variety of structures and currencies. Some lesser known names are the better risks.

- The market is relatively inaccessible to UK private investors, except indirectly through some corporate bond funds.

Corporate bonds

Most of this book has focused on investing in government bonds. Chapter 7 hinted at the fact that companies also issue bonds. Many US private investors invest in corporate bonds. In the UK they rarely do so directly. More likely they invest through a corporate bond fund. Some have found that funds like this are far from risk free.

Chapter 10 looks at the opportunities for collective investment in bonds through bond unit trusts, mutual funds and other open-ended investment companies. This chapter outlines the principles of investing in corporate bonds. It looks at the characteristics of corporate bonds and the risks they entail.

Why companies issue bonds

Bonds are not the uniform category that many investors suppose. As we noted in an earlier chapter, all shares are similar in concept and are issued by a wide variety of companies. In the bond markets there are fewer issuers, but more types of bond issued.

Issuers of bonds range from industrial companies through to banks, international agencies and governments. Bonds come in all shapes and sizes, including floating and fixed rates, high coupon, low coupon and zero coupon, short dated, long dated and undated, convertible and exchangeable, and in many other forms. What binds all bonds together is the way in which they are valued. As we have seen, this is on the basis of their redemption yield, the time value of money, the degree to which they are secured on specific assets, and their relative credit quality. The assessment of credit quality – making a judgement about the financial soundness or otherwise of the issuer – is particularly important in the corporate bond market.

> Issuers of bonds range from industrial companies through to banks, international agencies and governments.

Companies issue bonds in a variety of forms and for a variety of reasons. Common reasons for bond issues are:

■ for short-term working capital

■ to increase balance sheet leverage

■ to substitute for bank finance

■ to pay for acquisitions

■ because other capital markets are closed to them or too costly.

Commercial paper is the market in which companies issue short-term fixed income debt. They do this to help finance immediate working capital requirements and to even out peaks and troughs in the flows of cash in and out of the business. Commercial paper is a professionals-only market. It is comparable to the market in government bills. That is to say, it is issued at a discount and repaid at par, rather than bearing a coupon. It is of short duration, usually a matter of days, weeks or a few months at most. Finally and most crucially it is unsecured, exposing its buyers to the risk of default. Because of this, only the companies with top-notch credit ratings can issue it.

While companies can use sophisticated transactions in the futures and options markets to achieve the same ends, many companies use the bond markets to replace floating rate bank finance. Tapping the bond markets allows them to fix a rate of interest for a lengthy period ahead. It avoids the unpredictability of dealing with a bank. If times get tough, banks may seek to call in a loan, not renew an overdraft facility, or tighten their terms.

Management may also take the view, if they are optimistic about the company's prospects, that raising capital through a bond issue may be a better way of financing expansion. For one thing, it avoids asking share-holders for money and, since a bond's coupon is a fixed money amount, a bond will 'gear up' the returns to equity shareholders when the investment bears fruit.

This is a higher risk strategy, particularly in times of economic un-certainty, because gearing works both ways. In other words, having more fixed rate debt (and indeed more debt generally) in a company's balance sheet increases the potential volatility of profits in the future. Table 8.1 shows in simple terms why this is so.

From time to time companies issue bonds to pay for takeovers, although the reaction of the market to such moves is often adverse. Typically a company contemplating a large acquisition may propose terms entailing payment in cash, a larger amount payable either in shares or in a con-vertible bond, or a mixture of all three.

The advantage to a company of issuing convertible debt as part of the

Table 8.1 Gearing effect of bond interest in corporate profits

Scenario
Ruritania Widgets has 100m bond issue with a 6% coupon.
Sales are 150, on which it makes a 10% operating margin.
In the period in question sales fluctuate sharply, as shown.

	Year 1	Year 2	Year 3
Sales	150	200	100
Margin	10	10	10
Operating profits	15	20	10
Interest	6	6	6
Profit after interest	9	14	4
Percentage change in sales		33	−50
Percentage change in profits		56	−71

terms of a takeover is that the conversion feature reduces the level of fixed coupon which the company needs to offer on the debt. The conversion of the bond into the associated shares may not take place for a couple of years, by which time (so the theory goes) the company will have reaped the benefits of the takeover. If so, the issue of new shares to satisfy the conversion terms will be easily offset by the growth in profits that the takeover has generated.

Finally, and more cynically, convertibles are harder to value accurately and are certainly somewhat less volatile than the underlying shares might be. This allows the company to claim it is offering takeover terms that are relatively stable in value. However, ploys like these have been mounted so often that the market tends to see through them. Often it views them as smacking a little of desperation or subterfuge. It may brand the convertible (sometimes unjustifiably) as 'funny money'.

From time to time companies are forced to issue bonds in preference to equity. This is usually because the equity markets are unreceptive to any form of equity issue, or it may be that the market will only stand a share issue on terms so onerous as to make issuing debt a cheaper alternative. In short, unreceptive equity markets mean that shares could only be issued at a deep discount to the current market price. This means that more shares have to be issued to raise a given amount of capital, diluting their value.

The next section looks at the different types of bonds that companies issue and how they work. This is followed by an explanation of the role of credit rating agencies and the methods they use to work out the risks of particular bonds and their issuers.

S I D E B A R

Enterprise value and the cost of capital

Analysts use these calculations to see whether or not a company should issue equity or debt.

Enterprise value is the total value of the company, taking into account both the stock market value of its issued shares (market capitalization) and its debt. A company with an equity market value of £100m and debt of £50m would have an enterprise value of £150m.

Weighted average cost of capital is a composite measure of what a company's sources of capital actually cost. Continuing the example immediately above:

The cost of debt (the average coupon on a company's bonds) is weighted for the proportion that debt represents in enterprise value. Let's say this cost is 6%. Debt represents a third of enterprise value. So this 6% cost is given a 33% weighting in the cost of capital calculation.

Cost of equity is more complex. It is the risk-free rate of return plus a notional equity risk premium (usually held to be about 4%) adjusted for the relative volatility of the shares. The risk-free rate of return is normally taken to be the yield on an appropriate government bond. The risk premium is the amount by which, on average, equity returns have exceeded returns on risk-free assets. If shares tend to move up or down by a greater or lesser percentage than the market changes, this relative difference is used to adjust the risk premium accordingly.

Say, for example the risk-free rate is 5%, the equity risk premium is 4% and the volatility adjustment factor is 1.25. Cost of equity would be 10% (5 + 1.25 × 4). The cost of equity is then weighted for the percentage that equity market capitalization represents in enterprise value, in this case two-thirds of the total. The two weighted costs are combined to arrive at the weighted average cost of capital. In this case it would be one-third of 6% (2%) plus two-thirds of 10% (6.7%). The weighted average cost of capital in this simple example would be 8.7% (2.0 + 6.7).

This has a bearing on whether a company issues equity or bonds to raise capital. If the cost of issuing debt is less than the weighted average cost of capital, this should be the preferred option.

In this case issuing debt at a cost of 6% is cheaper than issuing equity, and will lower the weighted average cost of capital.

The corporate bond pecking order

Investors assess corporate bonds not only on the basis of their yield and the creditworthiness of the issuer, but also on the basis of their position in the pecking order for payment if there is a default. In simple terms, bonds are safer if they are secured on something specific, such as property or plant and machinery. Bond issue prospectuses contain information about the legal standing of bonds and the rights of bondholders in the event of a default. One feature is that bonds have trigger points, known as covenants, which may give extra power to debt providers – often including banks – to influence events if they are breached.

Covenants often relate to the cover for interest payments (the amount by which profits before interest exceed annual interest payments). Bondholders wish to see minimum levels of interest cover maintained in order to be sure that their interest will be paid in full and on time.

The pecking order differs from case to case, but it is important to be aware of distinctions. If a company is put into liquidation, assets are sold and the bondholders, bankers and other creditors have their claims satisfied in a strict order of priority. The order runs something like this:

■ *Debenture holders* have their principal amount and unpaid interest secured against specific assets, such as property, which can be sold to produce the necessary funds.

■ *'Senior' debt holders* have their claims satisfied next, from the remainder of the assets.

■ *Junior or 'subordinated' debt holders* have their claims satisfied from the remainder of the assets.

■ *Unsecured debt* issued by the company is satisfied next, if any funds remain available.

■ *Banks* may have a mixture of secured and unsecured debt. They are often the catalyst for liquidation or restructuring.

■ *Unsecured creditors* (including suppliers) rank next, although in many liquidations (as I know from personal experience!) frequently get little or nothing.

■ *Preference shareholders* rank ahead of ordinary shares.

It follows from this that the further up the pecking order you are, the safer your investment is from the impact of a default. In turn, the lower is the yield premium over a risk-free rate to make the investment worthwhile. The difference in yield between the bond with the most security and that with the least will vary with the issuer.

S I D E B A R

Samurais, bulldogs, yankees and matadors

In recent years, companies have taken advantage of the globalization of capital markets to launch bond issues in other countries' currencies, aimed at investors in those countries. For example, Deutsche Telekom might issue a bond denominated in yen aimed at Japanese domestic investors, or BT launch a bond in US dollars aimed at American investors. There are often good reasons for doing this. One reason may simply be lower rates of interest than in the home market. Another might be that the company is planning a major investment in the country and wants to match the asset to a liability of similar size.

Either way, the international bond market being what it is, bankers have coined evocative names for these bonds. Hence, a bond issued in sterling by a foreign borrower is known as a 'bulldog', a bond issued in dollars is a 'yankee' bond, a bond issued in yen is a 'samurai', and so on. The advent of the Euro-zone threatens to spoil a lot of the fun in this regard. Bonds issued by foreign borrowers in pesetas for Spanish investors used to be called 'matadors'. No term has yet been invented for bonds issued in Euros by outside issuers. 'Maastrichts', perhaps?

In a very solid company, a lower degree of security in a bond may seem academic, and so the spread between the most and least secure bonds is minimal. In a more financially stretched company there may be a big difference in yields between 'safe' bonds secured on specific assets and those that are unsecured and therefore more vulnerable to a potential default.

Differences in perceived credit quality also mean that even senior or secured bonds from a poor 'credit' might have higher yields than unsecured bonds from a top-rated firm. Defaults do happen, but often they are less open and shut cases for investors than the description above suggests. What sometimes happens (notably in the USA, but also to an increasing degree in Europe) is that in the event of liquidations or 'distress' situations, an informal market develops in the debt. This lets some bondholders pass on their claims to others at a discount, in return for a quick and uncomplicated exit. See the last section of this chapter for more on this phenomenon.

Corporate bonds for private investors

Private investors buying UK corporate bonds usually come across a limited number of different types. These are:

■ 'straight' bonds, including debentures and other secured credits

■ floating rate notes, issued as an alternative to cash in takeovers

■ convertible bonds, bought in the market or issued in takeovers.

As noted previously, debentures are the 'safest' form of corporate debt because they are secured on specific assets. While this is often property or property-related assets, occasionally the charge can be over something more unusual.

BOC, an industrial gases company, issued debt with interest payments guaranteed by revenue from its long-term contracts to supply its industrial customers and principal secured by a charge on the plant it used to produce these gases.

We covered floating rate notes in an earlier chapter. Companies often issue them as an alternative to a cash payment in a takeover situation, to allow investors in the target company to phase disposals for CGT purposes. It's important to remember that they are normally unsecured and so do bear some credit risk.

The more common type of corporate bond that investors may encounter is the 'convertible'. The full name is usually convertible unsecured loan stock (CULS). We looked at convertibles in brief in an earlier chapter. A CULS is a combination of a straight bond with an option to convert into the ordinary shares of the issuer on fixed terms and at a specific point in the future. At the time it is issued, the conversion terms usually mean that the option will only be worth exercising if the price of the underlying shares goes up by a significant amount from the current level.

The embedded option is therefore an out-of-the-money call option. A call option is an option to buy shares. It is out-of-the-money because the effective exercise price (the price at which conversion becomes worthwhile, according to the conversion terms) is above the current price of the shares. The shares have to move up for the option to be in-the-money – that is to say, worth exercising. The sidebar shows how an imaginary bond's term can be used to work out its value.

This simplified example demonstrates how to split convertibles into their component parts and value them separately. It also shows that they are essentially cautious investments. They give investors the security of a bond investment and a fixed return, as well as exposure to the underlying equity.

However, as the example shows, the conversion feature can represent a very small part of the bond. It produces a very diluted benefit even if the price of the underlying shares increases dramatically. In the example, a doubling in the underlying share price raises the total return on the bond from 5.25% to 11.75% (5.25% + 6.5%). In absolute terms the benefit is modest compared with having the entire £1000 investment in the underlying shares.

SIDEBAR

Valuing a convertible

Ruritania Electric 5% Convertible Unsecured Loan Stock 2007

The bond has a semi-annual coupon and matures on 30 June 2007. Each bond has a face value of £1000 and converts into 50 shares. The price of the underlying shares is 150p.

Step One: What are the bond's components? The convertible has two components – a straight bond with a 5% coupon and maturity date of 2007 and, assuming a price of 100, an out-of-the-money option to buy 50 shares with an exercise price of 200p (£1000/50).

Note: *if the price of the bond had been 110% the effective exercise price would have been higher, because the rights to the conversion into 50 shares would have cost £1100, not £1000.*

Step Two: Value the option component The option to convert is a call option with an expiry date of 30 June 2007 and an exercise price of 200p. Assuming the share's volatility is 20%, the value of the option is 30p per share, or £15 for the 50 shares involved in the bond. Volatility of the underlying shares is an important component of an option's price.

Note: *if the underlying price were to rise to 300p and everything else is unchanged, the value of the option rises to 156p per share, or £78 for the 50 shares involved.*

You can use any simple option valuation model to do these calculations – provided that volatility, exercise price and expiry date are known. In this calculation I used 'Optimum', which can be downloaded from Nigel Webb Software (www.warp9.org/nwsoft).

Step Three: Value the bond component Valuing the straight component of the bond requires that you make an assumption about the credit-worthiness of the issuer relative to the risk-free equivalent.

Assume that Ruritanian government bonds with the same maturity have a redemption yield of 4.75% and that normally the spread for Ruritania Electric is 50 basis points. The straight part of the bond should yield 5.25%, implying a price (calculated using a simple financial calculator) of 98.73%.

Step Four: Add the two components together The value of the bond at present on these assumptions is 987.3 + 15 or 1002.3, approximately a quarter point above par.

Note: *if the underlying share price were suddenly to rise to 300p, however, the convertible (other things being equal) would be worth 987.3 + 78, or 1065.3, a 6.5% premium to par value.*

An exchangeable bond is one where the bond is convertible into shares other than those of the issuer. An example was the recent France Telecom issue of bonds exchangeable into shares of Orange. This bond issue accompanied Orange's public share offer. Separating the bond into its component parts allows investors to value exchangeable bonds in exactly the same way as described above.

> An exchangeable bond is one where the bond is convertible into shares other than those of the issuer.

Many convertible bonds allow the issuer the option of redeeming the bond before maturity (this is known as 'calling'). A call provision shortens the window during which the option to convert the bond can be used and hence detracts from its value to the investor.

Bond issuers therefore have to guarantee a certain minimum period of time during which the bond can be converted. Or they may only call the bond if the underlying shares trade well above the conversion price for a certain length of time. A bond, for example, might only be callable after the underlying shares trade at more than 150% of the conversion price for 30 days.

Credit quality

Credit quality and the market's perception of it are vital to understanding the way the bond market functions and whether or not specific bonds are cheap or dear. In the stock market these days there are few authoritative independent voices conducting research into companies and appraising their shares. The bond market is somewhat different. It has a system that independently assesses both governments and companies on the basis of their financial soundness and their ability to meet the commitments their bonds entail.

Credit rating agencies conduct these assessments. While there is sometimes controversy over the way they function, they are independent of the investment banks that manage bond issues. This is an important difference from the equity market: equity analysts working for investment banks are now little more than highly paid cheerleaders and their objectivity is in grave doubt.

Credit rating agencies like Moody's and Standard & Poors conduct intensive research into would-be (or actual) issuers and assign each one a rating (AAA, AA, B, etc.) based on their credit quality. In the case of companies, the rating process involves both intensive financial and industry analysis supplemented by lengthy interviews with senior management. The rating agency reviews the rating periodically. It may upgrade or downgrade it depending on changes in the operating and industry background of the issuer, or changes in its financial condition. Among the factors reviewed are:

- industry trends
- the political and regulatory environment under which the company operates
- management quality and the company's attitude to risk taking
- its operating and competitive position
- its financial position and sources of liquidity
- accounting quality
- the company structure (especially relevant if the issuer is a subsidiary of a larger entity) and the degree to which it may be supported by its parent company
- various other issues.

While ratings and changes to them can be controversial, as Table 8.2 shows, the raters get it right more often than not. Default rates are a very low probability for large AAA-rated companies and increase gradually and then progressively further down the credit quality spectrum.

Table 8.2 Likelihood of default in different rating categories

Rating over (yrs)	Aaa AAA	Aa AA	A A	Baa BBB	Ba BB	B B
1	0	0.08	0.08	0.3	1.43	4.48
2	0	0.25	0.27	0.94	3.45	9.16
3	0.02	0.41	0.6	1.73	5.57	13.73
4	0.09	0.61	0.97	2.62	7.8	17.56
5	0.2	0.97	1.37	3.51	10.04	20.89
6	0.31	1.37	1.78	4.45	12.09	23.68
7	0.43	1.81	2.23	5.34	13.9	26.19
8	0.62	2.26	2.63	6.21	15.73	28.32
9	0.83	2.67	3.1	7.12	17.31	30.22
10	1.09	3.1	3.61	7.92	19.05	31.9
15	1.89	5.61	6.13	11.46	25.95	39.17
20	2.38	6.75	7.47	13.95	30.82	43.7

Note: The table shows the rating categories for Moody's and S&P. Data cover the period 1920–99. Over this period the figures show the percentage likelihood of some form of default in each category relative to the number of years a bond was held. Example: a B-rated credit had on average a 20.89% chance of experiencing a default during any five-year period.

Source: Moody's

Rating banks is a special subset of corporate credit rating. Moody's adopts a system with the acronym CAMEL, which stands for: capital, asset quality, management, earnings and liquidity. Among the features it looks for are: high capital adequacy ratios; diversification of loan portfolio and steady growth in loans; clearly stated credit policies; management with experience, honesty and integrity; high return on equity and return on assets; a stable income stream with few exceptional items; and a stable customer base.

Because of their pivotal role in the financial system, investors and regulators scrutinize bank ratings particularly closely. One reason for this is that what banks do often involves greater levels of risk than are sometimes the case for industrial companies. This is not just because the nature of the business (lending money to customers on the basis of private bilateral agreements) is necessarily opaque, but also because many banks have become more dependent on trading in share and bond markets to supplement their profits.

Rating banks sometimes gives rise to differences of opinion between rating agencies about their credit quality. This shows how difficult the rating process is. Banks gain particular value from their credit standing, because it has a material influence on their cost of finance. Unlike industrial companies, therefore, banks are usually much less ready to contemplate action that might adversely affect their credit standing. So what do the ratings mean? This is summarized in Table 8.3.

The awarding of credit ratings is not an academic exercise. It clearly has repercussions for companies that are habitual users of the bond market. Slipping down a notch or two in the pecking order of credit ratings means that investors will demand higher yields to compensate for the extra risk in holding the bonds. Companies will have to offer more generous terms to attract investors when making new bond issues. In turn this will raise the company's overall cost of borrowing.

> The awarding of credit ratings is not an academic exercise. It clearly has repercussions for companies that are habitual users of the bond market.

One important point is that any investor in corporate bonds faces what is called 'event risk'. This is the risk that a credit rating will be downgraded because of a particular event over which they have no control. This could, for instance, be an acquisition that worsens a company's finances. This undermines the position of those

Table 8.3   What the ratings mean

Rating	Meaning
AAA	Capacity to meet obligations is 'very strong'
AA	Differs from AAA only slightly
A	More susceptible to changes in conditions. 'Strong' rather than 'very strong'
BBB	Likely to be affected to changes in condition but protection 'adequate'
BB	Uncertainties may mean inadequate capability of meeting commitments
B	Uncertainties are likely to impair ability to meet commitments
CCC	Vulnerable to non-payment unless conditions improve
CC	Highly vulnerable to non-payment
C	Currently paying, but default highly likely
D	In default
NR	Not rated, or insufficient information

who have previously bought the company's bonds on the basis of its previous higher credit rating. A lower credit rating means a company's bonds will sell on a higher yield basis, and therefore that the price of bonds already issued will fall.

The most topical recent instance of this related to BT, formerly regarded as a top-quality borrower. In the wake of the sharp deterioration in the company's balance sheet strength following various acquisitions and the 3G licence payments, BT's credit rating fell from A to BBB. Quite apart from the damage that existing holders of BT bonds have suffered as a result, observers estimated the change could cost the company an annual £140m in additional interest payments.

Bondholders have responded to the problem of event risk by insisting, in the case of some recent corporate bond issues, on a measure of credit protection. This has taken the form of an automatic increase in the coupon on the bond if the credit rating of the company is downgraded. A recent so-called 'coupon step-up' in a France Telecom bond issue provided for a 0.25% increase in coupon for each notch below an A rating that either of the two major credit rating agencies applied subsequently.

> Bondholders have responded to the problem of event risk by insisting on a measure of credit protection.

Terms like this reflect investor unease in particular industries (telecoms is the obvious example). Here major consolidation is a continuing theme and pressure to buy up rivals in large corporate mergers can result in severely strained balance sheets.

The real point about credit ratings is that although they can and do change, it is the market's perception and anticipation of any changes that is important. Bond markets sometimes overreact – in both directions – to actual or predicted rating changes. When buying corporate bonds, investors have to make a judgement about several factors. This includes not only the likely course of the benchmark yield curve, but also the spreads appropriate for corporate bonds in general, and whether or not the yield spread for that particular issuer is too high or too low bearing in mind its underlying credit quality.

Investors have to decide whether the respective judgements of the market (embodied in the yield on the bond) and the rating agency (embodied in the credit rating) match reality. One or both of these may not. As easier way of explaining this dilemma is in the form of several questions to be asked and answered in turn. These are shown in Table 8.4.

Each of the factors in Table 8.4 can reinforce the others, or pull in an opposing direction. The balance of them determines whether or not the bond is cheap, expensive, or correctly priced. In the most extreme case,

Table 8.4 Key questions when assessing corporate bonds

1. What does the benchmark yield curve suggest is the next likely movement for bonds of this maturity?

2. Independently of the answer to question 1, are corporate bond spreads versus the benchmark at this maturity too high or too low?

3. Independently of the answers to questions 1 and 2, is the true credit quality of the issuer better, worse or in line with the credit rating assigned to it?

4. Bearing in mind the answer to question 3, is the market's view of the credit quality of the issuer too optimistic or too pessimistic?

for example, the yield curve may be about to shift down, corporate bond spreads may narrow as a result, the true credit quality of the issuer may be better than the rating suggests and the market may be taking too pessimistic a view of it. In this case, a correction of all these factors will produce a quadruple whammy and a sharp rise in the price of the bonds.

Junk bonds

At the bottom end of the tier of credit quality are so-called 'junk bonds', or by the less evocative term 'high-yield debt'. Junk is debt deemed to be

> **Junk is debt deemed to be below 'investment grade' by the credit rating agencies.**

below 'investment grade' by the credit rating agencies. In Table 8.3 this corresponds to anything rated BB or below. Ratings below 'investment grade' happen for a number of reasons. One may be that a perfectly normal company has a balance sheet that looks excessively strained. If so, the credit rating may drop to such a point that the bonds fall into the 'junk' bond category.

More normally, however, junk is understood to apply to the bonds of companies that have too short a track record to justify a credit rating. The bonds may simply have been issued for the purpose of allowing a financier to mount a takeover assault on a more established company. It was in this context that the junk bond was developed in the USA in the 1980s. Its originator was the investment bank of Drexel Burnham Lambert, or more particularly Michael Milken, one of its star employees. While there were many instances of small companies using junk bonds to expand their businesses successfully when conventional avenues of finance were denied them, the junk bond became better known as a weapon of corporate predators.

Personalities such as Carl Icahn, Sir James Goldsmith and others used junk bonds to mount takeover assaults on sleepy companies. They used the argument that the bonds' interest and principal could be paid out of the proceeds of restructuring and asset sales once the takeover was completed. In a sense the bonds were, at least informally, secured on the assets of the target company.

The junk bond market at this stage of its development was marked by a degree of opaqueness in the way such bonds were priced (since Drexel effectively controlled the market in many of them). What eventually happened was that Milken was implicated in the insider trading scandal surrounding Ivan Boesky and others on Wall Street and served a prison sentence for his role in it.

However, the venture capital community took to heart the idea behind high-yield bond financing. High-yield bonds have, for example, long been employed in the USA as one of the components in the financing of leveraged buyouts. These are where an investor group acquires a public company, or a division of a large company. The investor group often, but not always, includes existing management. In cases like these, the buyer issues high-yield debt to pay for the purchase, which is usually a company with stable cash flow. The technique is now increasingly used in Europe. Cigarette companies and food businesses are favourite targets for treatment of this sort. It has been used in Europe to finance cable TV businesses and telecoms operators (Table 8.5).

All this is of academic interest to most private investors, at least as far as buying such instruments directly is concerned. But some corporate bond funds do invest in debt like this. So awareness of how high-yield

Table 8.5 Selected information on European high-yield bonds

Company	Coupon (%)	Maturity	Rating	Yield (%)	Spread (%)
Colt Telecom	7.625	2009	B1	9.22	419
FME	7.375	2008	Ba3	7.68	247
Kappa Packaging	10.625	2009	B2	9.22	461
NTL	9.875	2009	B2	14.44	942
UPC	11.25	2010	B2	20.07	1504
William Hill	10.625	2008	B3	9.3	421

Sources: WSJE, Moody's

debt works, and why it is used, is important for investors. The high-yield aspect of debt like this means high risks too. A high proportion of venture capital and management buyout deals fail (perhaps as many as a third). So high-yield bond investors, and those who buy funds that invest in it, can suffer some loss of capital value through defaults. Careful selection, and spreading risk through diversification, reduces the likelihood of a major 'hit'.

Distressed debt

It is important for all investors to realize that defaults do happen, and it is instructive to examine what can happen when they do. In the USA and increasingly in Europe, what happens is that distressed debt traders buy the claims of bondholders. Often bondholders may wish to sell quickly. The reason is that they will often settle for a discount to face value rather than suffer the uncertainty over whether or not that they might be paid out in full in the future.

Trading of this type dates back more than a century. Distressed debt traders make money consistently. The reason is that often the price of distressed debt is unduly depressed. This is usually because of adverse sentiment (the stigma of potential bankruptcy), a lack of liquidity, or because there are forced sellers. Many big investors cannot hold defaulting bonds in their portfolio and must sell them if this looks likely.

Bonds often have a claim on the assets of the company. But the precise value of the claim may depend on the extent to which reconstructions are permitted, and the rights attaching to different types of bond. These differ significantly from case to case. Negotiation with banks and other creditors usually require active involvement. So a trader often has to buy enough of a particular type of debt to get a seat on the creditors' committee.

Patience can pay off. Creditors may not have the nerve to wait for a restructuring, pension funds may be barred from holding busted bonds, and banks may be keen to sell off their claims for cash to remove an embarrassing loan from their books. Distressed debt traders make money by buying at deep discounts from those who can't wait or don't want to wait for a restructuring to be completed. Ultimately it's another variant of the risk and return dichotomy that underlies all forms of investment.

IN BRIEF

- Companies often issue bonds because it is cheaper to do so, or because equity capital issues are difficult. Convertible bonds are often used as currency for takeovers.

- Other than convertibles, UK investors rarely buy corporate bonds directly. They are more likely to invest in a corporate bond fund (see Chapter 10).

- Credit quality is crucial to corporate bond investing. Rating agencies provide independent guidance on the financial soundness of issuers. Rating downgrades can have a serious adverse impact on the prices of a company's bonds.

- Corporate bond investors need to beware of 'event risk'. This is where management action contributes to a downgrade in the credit rating. Banks are less susceptible to event risk than industrial companies.

- Junk bonds (or high-yield debt) are bonds issued with credit ratings below BBB. They are used for aggressive takeovers and leveraged buyouts.

chapter nine

Bond market information and how to get it

Getting information about companies and share prices is comparatively easy. For bond investors the task is harder, but not impossible. There is information available on a wide range of bond market topics: the price of government bonds, Eurobonds and corporate bonds; information on bond funds; and information on the economic background that drives bond markets. You just need to know where to look. You can find information in both print and online forms, although the web is becoming more important as a source of information as time goes by.

Information on bond prices and credit ratings is important. But equally investors need to keep in mind that perceptions of the outlook for the major world economies – especially the outlook for US interest rates – drive both bond and stock markets. Nuances in speeches from Federal Reserve Chairman, Alan Greenspan, have a big effect on stock and bond markets. This means it is vital for bond investors to have a good understanding of what makes these big economies tick, when to expect major policy statements and the significance or otherwise of official statistics.

Bond prices and analysis

Investors looking for bond prices and other basic investment information may find it is less plentiful than share price data. But this is less of a handicap than it might seem. Bonds, or at least government bonds, trade in highly competitive markets with generally much narrower spreads than is the case in equity markets. There is less likelihood (though not complete certainty) in the bond markets of a private investor dealing in a government bond at the 'wrong' price. What matters more is analyzing the factors that drive bond market performance: yield curves; credit ratings; the economic background;

> Investors looking for bond prices and other basic investment information may find it is less plentiful than share price data.

the outlook for inflation; and the rate of return on competing investments.

Prices

Financial newspapers such as the *Financial Times* and *Wall Street Journal* provide a lot of information about their own domestic bond markets. The latter's European edition also carries information on US bond markets. The FT recently expanded its coverage of bond prices and scope of the information presented. As well as editorial coverage, the international capital markets page provides: price and yield information for all UK government bonds; FTSE actuaries government securities indices; yields on benchmark government bonds and some leading corporate issues.

There are also tables giving information on: the spreads of 10-year government bonds against US Treasuries and German Bunds; prices, yields and spread data on various Eurobonds and emerging market government bonds; and information on bond futures and options in leading markets. In addition these pages also contain guidance on the relative volatility of leading government bond markets versus their respective equity markets. This is measured by the standardized Riskgrade concept devised by Riskmetrics (see Figure 9.4, p. 154).

> **Monday's Financial Times includes details of interest payment dates and amounts outstanding for gilt-edge stocks**

Additional information available each week in Monday's *Financial Times* includes details of interest payment dates and amounts outstanding for gilt-edge stocks. All would-be bond investors should study the statistics available on these pages to get a view of how the bond markets of the world interlock.

On the web, things are not quite so easy. There are tables giving ticker symbols for most UK government bonds earlier in this book. In theory you can use these to obtain dealing prices. While information on government bonds can be found fairly easily, finding out the basics on other bond products is more troublesome. Many bonds are traded only in over-the-counter interbank markets and hence the availability of prices to the man in the street is very limited.

Prices of convertible bonds are, however, often shown alongside the relevant equity in newspaper share price tables. Some may also be available through conventional quote server systems on the web. Some investment software packages provide data on convertibles as well as equities.

Bonds are more homogeneous than equities. UK gilts are mainly called Treasury stock, Exchequer stock, Conversion stock and identified only by the coupon and maturity date. Some stock codes for these securities are more cryptic than most equities. Inserting the word Treasury, Exchequer (and so on) into a ticker look-up facility can help locate the code for the stock you want. You can then load ticker codes into a dummy 'portfolio' or 'watch list' at a financial portal such as Interactive Investor (www.iii.co. uk) or ADVFN (www.advfn.com) and monitor bond prices with greater ease (Figure 9.1).

Figure 9.1   ADVFN

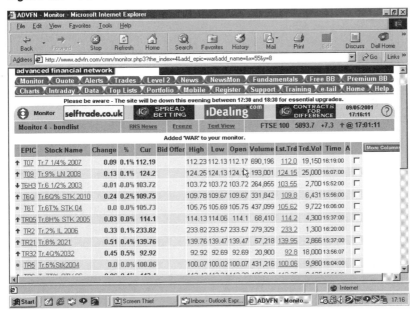

Investors face more of a problem with Eurobonds. Prices are often indicative, or simply unavailable. As noted earlier, ISMA may soon display some Eurobond price information on the web. Mostly, investors will have to resort to information provided by their bank or broker to get accurate prices.

Other sites have only a pale imitation of the detail provided on Bloomberg's pages (Figure 9.2). Quote.com (www.quote. com) does provide a page of quotes for the main US benchmark Treasury issues, as does Reuters (http://quotes.reuters.com). The lack of information on benchmark bonds in other markets is a surprising and disappointing omission at the Reuters site. Reuters does have a specialist bond site at Reuters Credit (http://credit.reuters.com) but this appears to be aimed at professional users and is subscription based. Users can register for a free trial.

Those spread betting or otherwise dealing in government bond futures and short-term interest rate contracts along the lines described in Chapter 4

Figure 9.2 Bloomberg

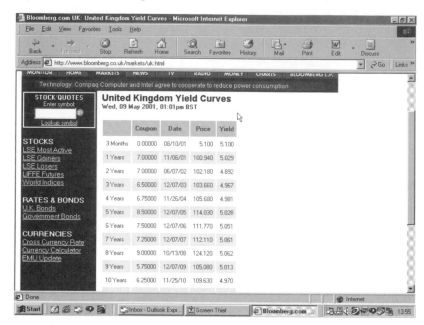

Bloomberg

Bloomberg is first and foremost a specialist provider of financial information for professional traders. Its founder, Mike Bloomberg worked as a bond trader at Salomon Brothers before starting it up. It's not surprising therefore that the Bloomberg site at www.bloomberg.co.uk is good for general information on bonds (Figure 9.1). It has several pages devoted to the bond markets. The site has a bond news page and a page giving prices and statistics for benchmark UK government bonds. The bonds included are not an exhaustive list, but the more actively traded ones.

Bloomberg also shows similar information for a wide range of other government bond markets around the world. It also has a wealth of news stories relevant to the bond markets. It has yield curve graphs for the US Treasury market but not for other jurisdictions, although it provides enough information for users to derive their own. You can do this by plugging the data into a spreadsheet and using the graph-drawing capabilities of a program like Excel (see later in this chapter for an explanation of how to do this).

are reasonably well served. There is a considerable amount of useful data at the respective derivatives exchange web sites. Information available includes contract specifications, prices, price histories and background research.

The best sources for data are probably LIFFE (www.liffe.com) for gilt and short sterling and Euro short-term interest rates, and Eurex (www.eurexchange.com) for all other Euro-zone bond derivatives. The CME (www.cme.com) has information on US-related, short-term interest rate derivative contracts and the CBOT (www.cbot.com) has data on US Treasury bond derivatives.

Bond background

Bond vocabulary is sometimes puzzling, but there are one or two points on the web that offer guidance. There is a list of books in Appendix 3 at the back of this book which provide good background information on bonds and bond terminology.

Kauders Portfolio Management, a specialist fund management firm dealing in UK government bonds, has a particularly good site, at www.gilt.co.uk. It has a useful collection of essays explaining the rationale for bond investing and the mechanics of undertaking it, together with a downloadable guide and examples of stocks suitable for particular classes of investor (Figure 9.3).

Figure 9.3 Gilt.co.uk

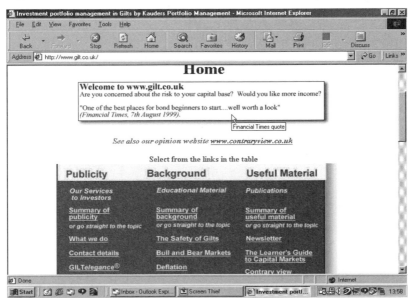

In all bond markets, borrowers are rated by specialist credit rating agencies. How these agencies work was described in the previous chapter and Chapter 3. To recap briefly, they assign borrowers a code letter in a strict pecking order based on various objective characteristics. Different rating agencies vary slightly in the codes they use and the rating criteria they apply.

Moody's website (www.moodys.com), for example, has brief comments on various topics. These include international bond market issues and also cover the US Treasury bond market. The comments are executive summaries of longer reports, although they are none the worse for that.

Other rating agencies are usually more generous in their provision of information for private investors. Standard & Poors, for example, keeps its most recent reports reserved for subscribers, but has an extensive archive of earlier research that is downloadable in PDF format. The web address is **www.standardpoor.com**.

Two other prominent firms – Fitch ICBA and Duff & Phelps – have now merged. The Fitch site provides extensive news and press releases on ratings topics. Once users have completed a (wholly free) registration process, they can view the reports in full. The coverage is particularly comprehensive. It includes 1000 banks and financial institutions, 400 companies and 50 nations. There are links to other relevant sites and news. The Fitch site is at the URL **www.fitch.com**.

Although the main thrust of these sites is US bond investors and issuers and national government bond markets, all three occasionally carry detailed reports on UK and European corporate bond issuers and industries. This is useful for investors. The methods by which the information is arrived at may be controversial, but these 'warts and all' reports about the individual companies' debt servicing capability make interesting reading. This is all the more so because they are prepared from a more dispassionate standpoint than most broker reports.

At the last count there were over 20 active rating agencies with a web presence, each of which provides a modicum of useful information for bond investors. The URLs of the best known are shown in Table 9.1.

There are a couple of other more general sites covering the bond markets as a whole. These are more US orientated, but nonetheless worth a look. One is Bond Resources (www.bondresources.com), which has some good educational material.

Investing in Bonds (www.investinginbonds.com) is a site organized by the US Bond Market Association. Despite its US bent and quasi-official status, it contains an excellent set of links to other bond-related resources.

Table 9.1 Rating agencies on the web

Company	Web address
AM Best	www.ambest.com
CBRS	www.cbrs.com
Capital Intelligence	www.ciratings.com
Fitch	www.fitch.com
Moody's	www.moodys.com
Standard & Poors	www.standardpoor.com
Thomson Bankwatch	www.bankwatch.com

Broker and bank research

Large investment banks seek to portray a caring public image. This is particularly true of those that have an extensive retail investor client base. A number of them allow reasonably unfettered access to their research on the web. Probably the best of these is JP Morgan, now part of the larger banking group of JP Morgan Chase. Morgan's site at www.jpmorgan.com has detailed data on global government bond markets. Information includes their size by nominal value and market value, the amounts in issue at various maturities, returns over time and volatility.

The published returns are a combination of the income yields on the bonds plus their price changes in local currencies and in dollars over the period. The data are stated in full. The site, as is normal, uses volatility as a proxy for risk. It shows how earning a higher return may often be accompanied by bigger than average price swings in the bonds. This is part of a wider research effort undertaken by the bank. The bank's research also includes analysis of emerging market government bonds and bonds issued by international bodies in the local currencies of emerging markets.

Taken as a whole this is an extremely useful resource for investors anxious to get some form of global perspective on bond markets. Anyone looking, for instance, to invest in the domestic government bond markets of any European country would do well to consult this site first. It's also worth remembering that JP Morgan set up the Riskmetrics organization. This company provides detailed risk management data for professional subscribers. In turn, Riskmetrics has spun out Riskgrades (www.riskgrades.com). This site caters to private investors. It provides standardized calculations of the relative riskiness of a range of securities, including bonds, and their relative risk when combined together in a portfolio (Figure 9.4).

Also worthy of comment is the Barclays Capital annual equity-gilt study, details of which are available from the firm's website at www.barcap.com.

Figure 9.4 Riskgrades

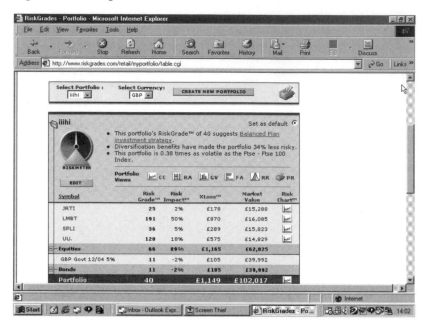

This publication is a comprehensive examination of the historic returns from bonds and equities over a lengthy timescale.

Interpretation of economic data is important for bond investors. This is as true for successful bond investment as it is for working out the economic background to an investment in a company operating in a particular territory. Expert analysts at securities firms, banks and other organizations devoted to economic research increasingly make their research available over the web.

Aside from the investment banks mentioned earlier, many UK broker websites post market commentary and economic analysis online. Around half of the UK brokers with websites appear to include some form of economic commentary on them. The provision of information like this changes, so check a few to find commentary you feel is valuable. There are links to the sites of some of these UK brokers at the APCIMS site (www.apcims.co.uk). A list of links to online brokers in the UK – some of which offer dealing in bonds – is at www.linksitemoney.com. The comments contained in some of these sites are sometimes restricted only to clients of the firm concerned. Others require would-be users to register and part with personal details.

In addition many of the comments are relatively superficial 'market reports' or else qualitative economic commentary written in the rather eccentric style that some UK brokers adopt. Rarely do they bear comparison with the rigorous analysis published (and sometimes made available free of charge over the web) by international banking groups and large US-owned investment banks.

A number of unit trust groups also publish comments on the economy and the markets. Around 40% of UK-based fund groups with websites publish information of this type. In general terms the comments are brief and cover a number of world markets.

News sites

There is an important role for newspapers and magazines in providing information on the bond market. This should not be forgotten. You can consult the print versions of these publications, but internet-enabled bond investors can log onto the respective websites. Print publications are sometimes superior for viewing tabular information relating to bond markets. Links to a wide range of newspapers, including financial journals and magazines, can be found at www.ajr.org.

Particularly useful are sites like FT.com (www.ft.com) where the archive can be searched easily for mentions of particular bond-related subjects, and FTMarketWatch (www.ftmarketwatch.com) for market data. *The Economist* (www.economist.com) has occasional thoughtful pieces on the role of the bond markets and likely trends in interest rates both in the UK and overseas. Would-be users need to subscribe to access the search facility.

The same is true of the *Wall Street Journal* (www.wsj.com) and *Business Week* (www.businessweekeurope.com). The WSJ is potentially the more useful of the two. Its print edition contains extensive bond market information. Forbes (www.forbes.com) and Kiplingers (www.kiplinger.com) both have useful tools for allocating and valuing bond investments. In the UK the *Investors Chronicle* (www.investorschronicle.co.uk) frequently runs articles with a bond and fixed income theme. Unfettered access to its site is reserved for subscribers.

Economic data and commentary

Given the importance of economic data to movements in bond prices, it is natural for bond investors to want information of this type, either in published form or online. The web is the most practical way to gain access to it. There is widespread provision of economic data on the web. As is the case with corporate websites, however, there are considerable variations in the way it is presented. The sources of statistics relevant for investors are typically – in OECD countries – the central bank of the country concerned and its national statistics collection and dissemination agency. A number of international organizations also provide statistical information.

Outside the OECD group, national statistics organizations typically provide the information. Even the smallest of countries have these. Rather like a national airline, having a national statistics organization with a website is a necessary concomitant of statehood. This is true even if (like a national airline) the service is poor and does little to enhance the country's standing.

General information sites

There are a few useful starting points for seeking out economic data relevant to bond market investment. One particularly good one is a resources page assembled by a technical university in Singapore at the web address www.ntu.edu.sg/library/statdata.htm. This is a simple but comprehensive collection of links. It is particularly good on Asia and the USA, but also contains links to many other statistics-related sites in the world. The US Census Bureau also has a page of links at its website. This gives access to the statistical agencies in most economies. The URL is www.census.gov/main/www/stat_int.html.

Central bank sites are often good sources of background information on national government bond markets and for relevant economic background. Many produce monthly bulletins, often with articles that are downloadable free of charge.

There are many private sector sites related to economics and economic statistics generally. Four are worthy of particular mention. The Dismal Scientist (www.dismal.com) takes its name from the nickname for economics as 'the dismal science' first coined by the philosopher and historian Thomas Carlyle. The site is one of the clearest on the web for identifying the timing of announcements and consensus expectations for major economic statistics. Much of the content is US orientated, but it covers other major world markets too – notably Japan and Germany. The site is non-technical, with a good page of classified links related to economics and statistics.

Ed Yardeni is chief economist at Deutsche Bank Securities in New York. His Yardeni Economic Network (www.yardeni.com) has a comprehensive selection of research and statistics available to the general public. Among the offerings is an archive of research notes (although the most recent are in a 'client-only' area). There are several pages of economic charts, mainly although not exclusively related to the US economy (Figure 9.5).

The Yardeni site also has a selection of links to statistics organizations on the web (although the list is far from comprehensive) and to economics

Figure 9.5   Yardeni

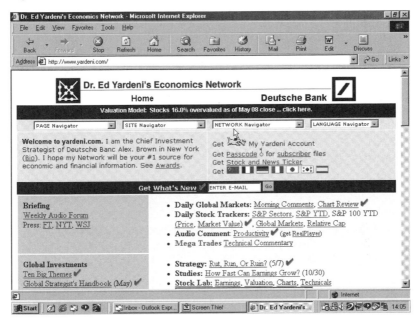

research, think tanks, central banks and other organizations. The site also contains links to newspapers, online research services and other sources of information. This is probably the best 'one-stop shop' on the net for economics information.

A good home-grown (for UK readers) site along similar lines is Lombard Street Research (www.lombard-st.co.uk). This is a consulting firm led by Professor Tim Congdon. The site has a number of publications available online (normally in PDF format) including a lengthy monthly commentary on economic matters. There are periodic daily notes commenting on recently released economic and financial statistics. Another section of the site comments in similar vein on economic statistics releases in other leading world markets. The text is brief and well written, accompanied by figures and graphs. This is one of the best of recently launched sites in this area.

Finally, Intermoney (www.intermoney.com) is part of the IdeaGlobal consultancy group. This site specializes in pithy analysis of economic data. It always makes clear its own views as well as those of the consensus, and why they differ. Some of the site is password protected. There is nonetheless enough information to allow users to get a good steer on the right numbers to look for in each successive official statistics announcement. The site also covers most major world bond markets.

Greenspan vs George

Central banks and national statistics organizations vie for attention when it comes to releasing information that bond markets view as sensitive. For easy availability of timely releases of important data to financial markets and investors, the USA stands head and shoulders above the rest. Having said that, statistical organizations proliferate within the USA, making access to the appropriate ones something of a chore.

The Federal Reserve's own news site is at http://www.federalreserve.gov. It has much additional information, including details of the Federal Reserve chairman's public speeches and evidence to congressional committees.

Other relevant government websites include the Bureau of Public Debt (www.publicdebt.treas.gov). It has a range of information about bonds issued by the US government and how to buy them.

The UK is generally somewhat less well served. Although some of the general sites mentioned above include information on the UK economy, official provision of statistics in the UK happens on a more piecemeal basis. The two key sources of information are the Office for National Statistics (www.statistics.gov.uk) and the Treasury web site (www.hm-treasury.gov.uk). The Bank of England site offers some interesting information (www.bankofengland.co.uk) and a recent redesign made its content more relevant to investors. The site has details of the minutes of the bank's monetary policy committee, responsible for setting interest rates in the UK. There are also details of speeches by bank officials and various working papers and other documents and statistics. The Debt Management Office (www. dmo.gov.uk) also has a website, although the content is of limited interest to most investors.

The Treasury site has a sizeable quota of resources of relevance for investors. These include ministerial speeches. A particularly interesting section for bond investors gives a detailed comparison of the forecasts made by the independent forecasters who publish analyses on the UK economy. This table provides a useful guide to the broad expectations of leading 'expert' forecasters.

Investors can register to receive press releases direct from the Treasury as they are issued. You do this by subscribing to an email list. Sadly, this is 'read only' and investors are unable to reply with comments on Treasury policy! Details of how to subscribe are at the Treasury site in the heading 'other useful information'. Whether or not you feel it worth subscribing to this list depends on how interested you are in the minutiae of economic policy. Many of the releases are mundane. They relate to the nuts and bolts of government policy and are not confined to material of direct interest to financial markets.

Looking at other major markets, the European Central Bank is the best source for economic data for the Euro-zone. Its website (www.ecb.int) has improved markedly since the early days, so much so that it has since won awards for the depth of its content. This includes: archived press releases, with a separate section for statistics releases; a calendar of future announcements; speeches from officials; links to EU central bank sites; and a range of other data.

Completing the picture for Japan, the Bank of Japan also has a website (www.boj.or.jp/en/) with an excellent range of content in English. This includes: reports and statistics; research papers; speeches; a schedule of future releases; and a special section from where reports and voluminous statistical data can be downloaded.

Aids for bond market mathematics

At one time calculating redemption yields required large and expensive books that tabulated yields for every possible combination of coupon, price and maturity date. There may be times when you don't want to trust the yield calculations published in daily papers, or else the bond you want to buy isn't listed there. If so, the big books are not necessary. A financial calculator will handle the necessary computation. Redemption yields are the easiest to calculate. The example in the sidebar uses a Texas Instruments BAII Plus.

This process seems cumbersome, but once accustomed to the work-sheet functions it is probably quicker than entering data into one of the online calculators described later in this section. The drawback is that the information available is limited to redemption yield and accrued interest. Projected bond prices can be calculated for a given redemption yield.

A conventional spreadsheet program is another useful aid for bond market investors. For example, you can use the chart facility in a program like Excel to produce a yield curve. First, create a simple worksheet with one column showing years to maturity from zero to 30 and a corresponding column for the redemption yield on the benchmark bond corresponding to that maturity. Benchmark bonds for particular years are shown in the *Financial Times* 'UK gilts – cash market' table in bold type. Use the current base rate, or the benchmark bond maturing in the current year, for the 'year 0' entry.

Table 9.2 shows the way the table would look calculated at the time of writing (mid-March 2001). It's worth bearing mind that at the longer end of the curve there are gaps. There is a benchmark bond for each year up to year 10 and then for years 15, 20, 25 and 30. In the UK's case at the

S I D E B A R

Calculating a redemption yield using a financial calculator

The sequence of steps required goes something like this (with keypad or display parameters highlighted in bold):

1 Enter the bond worksheet by pressing **2nd** and **Bond**.

   Move between fields by pressing up or down arrows. Enter data using **ENTER** key and calculate values by pressing **CPT** (compute).

2 Enter settlement date (**SDT**). This will normally be indicated by the broker at the time of purchase and varies from country to country. Normally add three or five working days to present day. Dates are input in the form dd.mmyy (10 March 2001 = 10.0301).

3 Enter coupon (**CPN**).

4 Enter redemption date (**RDT**). This should be entered precisely, that is down to the actual day in the format described above.

5 Enter redemption value (**RV** – normally = 100).

6 Alter (if necessary) day count convention (**ACT** or **360**). The calculator offers either actual/actual or actual/360. Setting the variable is accomplished by pressing **2nd** and **Set** alternately, while in the appropriate field.

7 Alter (if necessary) coupon payment frequency. The calculator defaults to twice yearly (displayed as **2/Y**).

8 Enter price (**PRI**), move to yield (**YLD**) and press compute to obtain redemption yield.

OR

9 Move to yield (**YLD**), enter yield and move to price (**PRI**) and press compute to obtain the price indicated for a given yield.

10 Move to **AI** to view accrued interest payable or receivable at current settlement date. This is calculated automatically.

Table 9.2 Graphing yield curves in Excel

	Redemption yields %	
Years to maturity	UK	USA
0	5.24	3.5
1	5.18	3.6
2	5.15	3.7
3	5.12	3.8
4	5.09	4
5	5.06	4.2
6	5.02	4.4
7	4.98	4.5
8	4.87	4.6
9	4.77	4.7
10	4.73	4.9
11		
12		
13		
14	4.75	5.3
15		
16		
17		
18		
19		
20	4.61	5.7
21		
22		
23		
24		
25		
26		
27	4.46	5.8
28		
29		
30		
31	4.39	5.9

Note: Yield data taken in mid-March 2001

time of writing, the benchmarks are at years 14, 20, 27 and 31. Appropriate gaps should be left in the spreadsheet to make sure the curve is not distorted. Leave yield entries blank for missing years. Do not enter zero!

Create the chart by highlighting the yield column and clicking on the chart wizard in Excel. Axes should be labelled 'redemption yield' and 'years to maturity' accordingly. The end result is shown in Figure 9.6.

Add data from different markets (perhaps using the Bloomberg site, which presents this in a standardized form) to compare the shape of the curve with those of other countries' bond markets. In this case the graph compares the (upward-sloping) UK yield curve with that of the USA.

Where basic spreadsheets and financial calculators fall down is in their inability to handle more complex questions. This is true even for a calculation as relatively simple as working out a bond's duration. There are, however a number of web-based bond calculators or downloadable software programs that allow these calculations to be performed either free of charge or inexpensively. For example, the website at www.financenter.com has a range of calculators. These can provide the answers to key bond-related questions such as those outlined below:

- Which bond is the better buy?
- What is my yield to maturity?
- What might be my yield if the bond is called early?

Figure 9.6   Yield curve

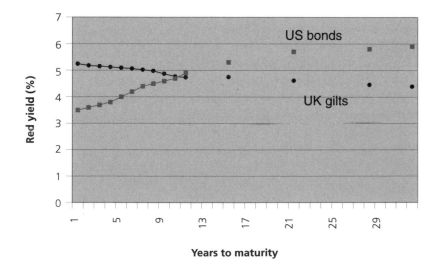

- What is the current running yield on the bond?
- Should I buy a zero-coupon bond?
- Which is better: discounted price or high coupon?
- How will rate changes affect a bond's current price?
- Should I sell before or after one year?
- What's my return if I sell today?
- What selling price guarantees my desired return?

The advantage of using this site is that, while some of the calculators are specifically designed for US investors, many are universally applicable. The site displays both answers and an explanation of why the calculations work as they do.

There are other sites that offer simple redemption yield calculators. Among them are Calculatorweb. The location of the bond calculator page is www.calculatorweb.com/calculators/bondcalc.shtml. This product allows you to specify coupon and maturity date. It then computes either price or yield. An interesting feature is that both price and yield entries have slider bars. Assume, for example, that yield drops by a percentage point. By moving the slider bar you can see instantly what impact this has on the price of the bond. Another site with a simple java-based calculator is www.longbond.com.

Cheap software for calculating bond variables is rare. One good product, which costs $25 for a registered version, is Compoundit! You can download it from www.bondsonline.com or normal download sites like www.download.com. There is a demo version, but it has limited functionality. It will not accept fractional prices or coupons. The file size, at 650Kb, is compact and downloads quickly. The software is easy to use. It will calculate yield to maturity, yield to call, duration and other parameters. It also supports several bond formats and day count conventions. The developer can be emailed at compoundsolutions@ibm.net.

There is some commentary on the web offerings of fund managers running corporate bond funds at the end of the next chapter.

IN BRIEF

■ Information on bonds is less easily available than for shares, but not that difficult to find.

■ Financial newspapers are some of the best sources of information on bond yields, bond prices and spreads.

■ Information on government bonds is easiest to find, that on Eurobonds the hardest.

■ There is extensive information available on the web about economic data relevant to bond markets. Sources include central banks, statistics organizations and private sector sites, including those of investment banks.

■ Calculators and software can make light work of computing yields and displaying yield curves and other information. There is a range of web-based calculators and cheap downloadable software.

chapter ten

Collective investments in bonds

U p to this point in the book we have looked only at direct investment in bonds. Many investors, however, opt to invest in bonds through a collective investment. Collective investments are funds for private investors run by professional managers. They include unit trusts and other so-called open-ended investment companies (OEICs). In the USA collective investments like this are called mutual funds.

> Collective investments are funds for private investors run by professional managers.

Unit trusts

What they are and how they work

Investment management companies operate unit trusts. They take in money from investors in exchange for units in a fund. The fund invests, at the discretion of the manager, in a predetermined way. The more money flows in from investors, the more units are created, the bigger the fund. Unit trust managers calculate the price of the units daily. The basis of calculation is the value of the fund's portfolio divided by the number of units. Investors can cash in units through the manager as they wish at the prevailing price.

The value of units can therefore rise and fall on the basis of the underlying performance of the fund's portfolio: investors buying or selling of units has no real effect on its underlying price. This is in marked contrast to investment trusts. These are closed funds whose shares have a stock market listing. The trust's share price can therefore move independently of the underlying value of the fund. It may stand at a discount or (occasionally) a premium to its underlying value. A unit trust's price, by contrast, is always an exact reflection of the fund's value.

Open-ended investment companies (OEICs) are similar in concept to a unit trust but conform to European financial services legislation. In theory this allows them to be marketed to investors across the EU. From the standpoint of the investor, the main difference between unit trusts and OEICs is that instead of separate bid (selling) and offer (buying) prices, an OEIC has a single price irrespective of whether investors are buying or selling units.

The fund management company running the fund compensates for the loss of the spread by economies in marketing and in higher charges. Some funds previously set up as unit trusts have converted into OEICs. In some instances management groups have merged several trusts into a new vehicle to achieve a larger, more cost effective fund.

Investing in unit trusts tax-effectively

> Many UK investors have come to own unit trusts through the medium of PEPs or ISAs.

Many UK investors have come to own unit trusts through the medium of Personal Equity Plans (PEPs) or their successors, Individual Savings Accounts (ISAs). These are 'wrappers' that can be put round existing funds to improve their tax efficiency. An investor can have a holding in a fund, with some of it as ISA or PEP, some of it as part of a personal pension, and a further holding as an ordinary investment.

If investors hold on for the appropriate length of time, gains made in PEPs and ISAs are tax free. Investors can receive tax-free income at any time, or alternatively reinvest it in the fund. Unlike an investment in a personal pension fund or an Enterprise Investment Scheme, however, ISA investors do not get a tax deduction on the amount invested.

The drawback to ISAs (and to PEPs before them) is that some of the tax advantages are swallowed up by charges. Some funds impose a hefty one-off initial charge (often in the region of 3–5% of the amount invested). On top of this, all funds usually have an annual management fee based on the amount invested. This is often around 1%, and sometimes more. Funds with high charges are not necessarily bad value. It may be worth paying them if the fund appears to have generated superior performance in the past.

The problem is that there are no guarantees that good performance will continue. Fund managers may change jobs within an organization or move to a new firm, or simply make mistakes. But a solid past track record with a modest initial charge may be preferable to investing in an unproven fund with an unknown manager, even if it has no initial charge. The best of both worlds of course are established funds that also offer low charges.

While it was originally intended that PEPs would only invest in the UK equity (i.e. shares) market, the rules were subsequently relaxed. The relaxations meant that PEPs could be used to invest in bonds and other fixed income stocks, and also in foreign stocks and bonds. This continued into the ISA regime. ISA rules are more convoluted in terms of the amounts that can be invested. ISAs can take in cash savings, as well as investments in life assurance, in addition to conventional securities. In their most straightforward form, a so-called 'maxi' ISA allows an individual to invest £7000 in any tax year. The investor does this either by selecting or transferring specific shares (a self-select ISA), or through investing the amount in a unit trust.

One particularly attractive aspect of the PEP and ISA regime has been that it allows investors to reinvest gross (i.e. untaxed) income in the fund. This allows – other things being equal – the capital value of the investment to increase with no tax penalty. This is particularly worth bearing in mind when it comes to funds that offer a high yields, such as bond funds.

It's worth bearing in mind, for example, that a yield after charges of 7%, if reinvested, will produce a doubling in capital value over a ten-year period. If you want proof of this, simply multiply 1.07 by itself nine times on a calculator: the end result is close to 2. A lot of the gain comes in the last few years, as Table 10.1 shows.

Table 10.1   Impact of 7% gross yield on £1000 compounding over 10 years

End of	Capital
Year 1	1070
Year 2	1145
Year 3	1225
Year 4	1311
Year 5	1403
Year 6	1501
Year 7	1606
Year 8	1718
Year 9	1838
Year 10	1967

Bond funds in general

Advantages and drawbacks

Any unit trust undergoes rises and falls in value. The extent of these fluctuations depends on the overall performance of the markets in which the manager invests, and the astuteness or otherwise of the selections he or she makes.

> Any unit trust undergoes rises and falls in value.

Bond funds are no exception to this rule. This is one crucial difference between investing in a bond fund and investing in a particular bond. If you buy a bond and hold it to maturity the redemption yield at the time you buy represents the annual compound total return you receive over the bond's life. This is particularly so in the case of a government bond, such as a UK gilt, where the risk of default is negligible.

With a bond fund, even one that invests in government bonds, there is no such guarantee. There is no fixed redemption date when the investment will be repaid at face value, and no guaranteed income. The capital value of the investment in the fund may go up or down in the meantime, depending on the decisions of the manager and the progress of the market.

Armed with the information in this book, it may be easier and more tax effective for an investor to create his or her own government bond fund. You can do this simply by buying gilts of the appropriate maturity and placing them within the tax-free wrapper offered by a self-select ISA. In doing this, you get a precisely tailored investment that has minimum levels of charges. Brokers charge for administering self-select ISAs, but charges tend to be low. The reason for doing this is because of a big disadvantage entailed in collective investments in gilts. It is that capital gains on gilts are tax free, whereas gains made in a gilt unit trust will not be, unless the fund is held in an ISA.

> Caution about potential fluctuations in capital value is particularly warranted when it comes to investing in corporate bond funds.

Caution about potential fluctuations in capital value is particularly warranted when it comes to investing in corporate bond funds. Management groups marketed corporate bond funds enthusiastically to ISA investors in the 1998–9 tax season. There were warnings about possible erosion of capital value in the small print. But the thrust of the advertising was headline yields that looked good against those offered by building societies or banks, and limited risk.

The capital values of many corporate bond funds contracted sharply in the following year. This was partly because yield spreads over government bonds widened in response to concerns over credit quality among issuers. But it was also because in some funds high headline yields could only be offered by buying high-coupon bonds above their par value. Many ISA investors subsequently deserted bond funds in the following year to invest in technology funds. They were just in time for an even more dramatic collapse in the value of these investments.

With the proviso that high yields may not always be what they seem (and may be stated before deducting charges) corporate bond funds do offer investors significant benefits in at least three particular respects:

- the individual manager's skill
- a lower level of risk through diversification
- access to bond markets normally closed to private investors.

Bond markets can be highly technical. Experienced managers can have an edge over the amateur, especially when it comes to maximizing income and avoiding risk. Even if you can select and buy corporate bonds on your own account, buying units in a fund will probably mean you have greater diversification and hence a lower level of exposure to any single bond. This is important in corporate bonds, where defaults can happen.

Finally, some markets may effectively be inaccessible to all but the wealthiest private investor. It would be unusual, for example, for UK investors to buy Eurobonds, but there are funds that allow a hassle-free way of gaining exposure to them, as well as the added advantages of manager skill and diversification.

As the experience of some corporate bond fund investors has shown in the past couple of years, even these attributes do not mean that funds like this are risk free. Would-be bond fund investors need to think carefully about a number of different factors when choosing a fund. Part of this decision-making process is bound up with whether or not bonds as a whole are the correct investment at that stage in the market cycle. Assuming that an investment in bonds looks right, the decision tree has several branches:

- government or corporate bond
- UK, overseas or a mixture of the two
- yield versus volatility
- take income or reinvest it
- tax-free wrapper or not

- the manager's record of past performance
- likely charges and their justification or otherwise.

None of these factors is mutually exclusive. Some funds may invest in both government bonds and corporate bonds. Some may allow income to be reinvested or for it to be paid on a regular basis into your bank. You may be prepared to accept the risk of a more volatile fund, or one with high charges, if the manager is particularly experienced. The ultimate choice of fund may rest on a mixture of these different factors, depending on your priorities. Not all funds can be placed in an ISA.

Specific fund choices and profiles

> Getting information on funds and fund performance is easier than it once was, particularly for investors with internet access.

Getting information on funds and fund performance is easier than it once was, particularly for investors with internet access. The previous chapter looked at sources of bond-related information on the web. Later in this chapter we examine government bond funds and corporate bond fund information available at the websites of unit trust managers. These vary considerably in quality.

For the purposes of compiling some statistics for this chapter, we looked at the range of funds on which information was available at Trustnet (www.trustnet.com). This is a specialist site covering unit trusts and other investment funds. It provides information about the funds' performance, composition of portfolios and other features. Detailed information on bond funds covers about 90 funds from a range of management groups. It includes 17 straightforward gilt-edge funds, with the remainder mainly or wholly invested in corporate bonds. There are more bond funds than this around, but some do not supply Trustnet with full information.

The funds highlighted later are simply examples, not recommendations. Readers should do their own research before investing in a fund. It is important, having picked a fund that seems appropriate for your needs, that you obtain (either online or by post) the literature relating to the fund's key features and past performance. Pay particular attention to the fund's performance, its portfolio exposure, charges and the experience of the manager. All of the examples, and the conclusions drawn, are based on data at the time of writing (March 2001). They are illustrative only. Numbers may have changed since then.

Government bond (gilt) funds

The section identifies several government bond funds that can be used in an ISA. As Table 10.2 shows, the managers are Thesis, Framlington, Aberdeen Asset Managers and Guardian. All have a significant initial charge of at least 3%. Annual charges vary between 0.75% and 1.75%.

Of the funds mentioned in Table 10.2, the best performing one appears to be Guardian's. Overall best performing gilt fund at the time of writing – at least on the basis of its percentage return over five years – was the Fleming Select Long Dated Gilt. The Merrill Lynch Long Dated Sterling Bond Fund was next, followed by the Gartmore Fixed Interest fund and the M&G Gilt & Fixed Interest. Gartmore had no less than five top performing funds in the top 20 over five years; Fleming had three.

Yields on gilt funds vary considerably. The highest yielding funds claim to offer 5–6%. In terms of capital accumulated, the top-performing fund returned more than 70% over five years and the top three more than 50%. British government securities as a whole showed 13% growth over five years.

Of those mentioned in Table 10.2, the Thesis fund is comparatively new. It appears to have a more eclectic investment policy than simply holding UK government bonds. The manager is David Tyerman. Trustnet contains little information on its portfolio holdings.

By contrast the Framlington Gilt Trust, managed by Laurent Hirsch, is unequivocally invested in a range of gilts and nothing else. It has shown appreciation of more than 30% over five years.

The Aberdeen Gilt Fund, managed by Rod Davidson, has a performance record dating back less than three years. At the time of writing it held just seven gilts, mainly short and short-medium maturities with relatively high coupons.

The Guardian Gilt & Fixed Interest fund appears to have a relatively diverse investment policy and has performed well over five years. There is little information on Trustnet about its portfolio. Steven Parrish is the fund's manager. It gives priority to capital preservation and secure income.

Mainstream corporate bond funds

For this section we tried to identify corporate bond funds that could be used in an ISA and which had no initial charges. No restrictions were placed on where the funds invested. The funds include some wholly invested in sterling bonds, as well as some with Eurobond and high-yield bond investments (Table 10.3).

Table 10.3 shows those thrown up by the database. Of these, only the

Table 10.2 ISA-able gilt funds

Name	Management group	Fund type	ISA	Initial charge	Annual charge	UK bonds	Cash savings plan	URL
Gilt fund	Aberdeen Asset Managers	UK open ended inv.	Yes	3.0	0.75	98	2 Yes	www.aberdeen-asset.com
Gilt trust	Framlington Unit Management	UK unit trust	Yes	3.0	1.0	95	5 Yes	www.framlington.co.uk
Gilt and fixed interest trust	Guardian Unit Managers	UK unit trust	Yes	3.5	1.5	100	Yes	www.guardianfs.co.uk
Thesis high income fund	Thesis Unit Trust Management	UK unit trust	Yes	3.0	0.75		No	n/a

Table 10.3 ISA-able corporate bond funds with no initial charges

Name	Management group	Fund type	ISA	Initial charge	Annual charge	Govts	Corporate bonds	Other	Savings Plan	URL
S&P High Income Fund	Chase Fleming Asset Management	UK unit trust	Yes	0.0	1.0	13	82	5	Yes	www.chaseflemingam.co.uk
Money Builder Income Fund	Fidelity Investment Services	UK open ended inv.	Yes	0.0	0.7	5	93	2	Yes	www.fidelity.co.uk
Higher Income Plus Fund	Norwich Union Investment Funds	UK open ended inv.	Yes	0.0	1.0		57	43	Yes	www.norwich-union.co.uk
AAA Income	Standard Life Investments (Mutual Funds)	UK open ended inv.	Yes	0.0	1.0	93		7	Yes	www.standardlifeinvestments.co.uk
Corporate Bond Fund	Woolwich Unit Trust Managers	UK unit trust	Yes	0.0	1.25				Yes	www.woolwich.co.uk

Source: Trustnet

Chase Fleming S&P High Income fund featured in the top performers over five years. This underlines a point made earlier. In corporate bond investing, the skill needed by investment managers to put together a top-performing portfolio can justify higher charges. Aberdeen Asset Management had two funds in the top three, Aberdeen Sterling Bond and Aberdeen Fixed Interest. Paul Reed, a doyen among UK fixed interest fund managers, manages both funds.

Investors incur significant initial charges when buying these funds 'retail'. Charges like this can sometimes be mitigated or avoided if the bonds are bought through fund supermarkets. Overall, the best performing corporate bond fund is the ABNAmro High Income Fund. This fund has risen 77% in value over five years.

The funds in the table of 'no-load' ISA friendly funds, however, are a disparate bunch. An outside manager runs the Woolwich Corporate Bond Fund. It has risen 38% over five years. No portfolio details are available, but the investment policy appears to be primarily UK orientated.

Ian Spreadbury manages Fidelity's longstanding Moneybuilder Income fund. It has almost entirely invested in UK or sterling denominated corporate bonds, generally those of larger companies. It has risen about 33% over five years.

Standard Life's AAA Income has been going less than three years. It has mainly invested in sterling denominated Eurobonds issued by a range of European companies. There is a mixture of maturity dates. Its ten largest holdings account for about four-fifths of the portfolio. They look very sound in terms of credit quality.

Chase Fleming's S&P High Income fund has been around for many years. It has risen by over 40% over five years. It has a disparate portfolio including some foreign bonds, but is mainly focused on UK names. It is managed by Peter Clelland.

Finally Norwich Union's Higher Income Plus OEIC had been around about a year at the time of writing. Roger Webb is its manager. It has a slightly racier profile than some. About 60% of the portfolio is in UK investment-grade corporate bonds, a further 28% in UK and about 9% in European high-yield debt. There is a good spread of maturities among its investments. As befits a portfolio of higher risk bonds, it is widely diversified. The largest holding accounts for only 2.4% of the portfolio, and the top ten make up about 21% of the total. This fund and the corporate bond sector lead on to a couple of general points.

The first point is that it may be necessary and even desirable to pay bigger fees to invest in the funds run by better performing managers. There is a premium in this area for astuteness and demonstrable experience.

Second, don't just look at headline yield. It pays to look at the portfolio underlying it. Have a glance at the top ten holdings in the portfolio, the degree of risk they seem to imply, the degree of concentration in the holdings, and the way the fund categorizes them in terms of geographical origin and credit quality. If the fund management group does not disclose these breakdowns, then remember you are buying blind, which can be risky.

Funds with broad geographical spread

Table 10.4 shows a list of funds that invest in a broad spread of government bonds. In some cases they also include high-quality Eurobonds. These funds have built decent performance records over a five-year period, with a minimum return of about 15%, and in some cases as high as 25% or 30%.

Table 10.4 proves the point that the broader the spread, the more insulated you will be from secular trends in any one country. This reduction in risk is at the expense of returns that tend to be lower than the star performers of the moment. The portfolio details of the funds in Table 10.4 can be sketched in briefly. The Newton International Bond Fund, managed by Helena Morrissey, is well spread geographically between the USA, UK and Europe. The fund has a large holding in an extra-long German government bond matched by a mix of maturities elsewhere, notably in the USA. This fund has notched up a 30% gain over five years.

The Old Mutual Worldwide Bond Fund, managed by Bob Attridge, has a similar performance. It is more heavily concentrated in Euro-zone government bonds (54% of the total) with the next biggest concentration (27%) in the USA.

The Merrill Lynch Global Bond Fund, managed by Peter Geikie-Cobb, has recorded a five-year performance of 20–25%. Euro-zone bonds make up 40% of the portfolio: the UK and USA are 25% each. Maturities are primarily in the 5–10-year range.

Finally, Derek Bartlett's City Financial International Capital Accumulator has also seen a 30% plus five-year performance. This differs from some of the other funds in several respects. First, it is an OEIC rather than a unit trust. Second, its portfolio is wholly in government bonds, and includes several large holdings of zero-coupon stocks. At the time of writing, six of the top ten holdings were zeros. Because of the nature of interest rate strips, this fund's portfolio is more sensitive to movements in interest rates than many others.

All of these mini-profiles demonstrate that the bond fund market is far from being as uniform as it appears at first sight. It means you need to take care when picking a fund. Make sure it is managed to your liking and that it has a portfolio with which you are comfortable.

Table 10.4 Broadly spread ISA-able bond funds

Name	Management group	Fund type	Initial charge	Annual charge	UK bonds	European	US bonds	Convs	Other	Savings plan	URL
High Yield Bond Unit Trust	Aberdeen Asset Managers	UK unit trust	4.25	1.25	45	28	10	16	1	Yes	www.aberdeen-asset.com
Aberdeen Global Champions Fund	Aberdeen Asset Managers	UK unit trust	4.25	1.25	45	28	10	16	1	Yes	www.aberdeen-asset.com
Barclays Global Investors Int Fixed Interest	Barclay Funds	UK unit trust	3.25	0.75	19	19	19	0	43	No	www.barclays.co.uk
Gerrard International Bond & Convertible Fund	Gerrard Investment Funds	UK unit trust	5.0	1.0	16	19	44	4	36	No	www.gerrard.com
Merrill Lynch Global Bond Fund	Merrill Lynch Fund Managers	Uk unit trust	5.0	1.0	24	48	11	0	17	Yes	www.mlim.co.uk
International Bond Fund	Newton Fund Managers	UK open ended inv.	4.0	1.0	10	32	30	0	28	Yes	www.newton.co.uk
Royal & Sun Alliance Worldwide Bond Trust	Royal & Sun Alliance Investments	UK open ended inv.	5.0	0.75	10	48	26	0	16	Yes	www.rsainvestments.com

Source: Trustnet

Bond fund management groups' websites

Trustnet and other similar sites, including UK fund supermarkets such as those operated by Egg (www.egg.com) and Fidelity (www.fundsdirect. co.uk), are not the only source of information on bond funds. Individual asset management groups have increasingly moved to put fund details on the web. Fund management groups were among the earliest to do this, but few convincingly embrace 'e-business'. This could be because there are strict regulations governing how products like this are advertised and sold to investors. Nonetheless the best of fund management sites show what can be achieved. If the will were there, the rest would emulate the design features which the best firms employ.

This section and the next look at fund management group sites from the standpoint of their user friendliness and the ease of getting at the information available. In compiling the database from which this assessment was made, we looked for a range of different features: whether sites provided fact sheets on their funds; whether there were details of the fund manager's experience; whether performance data were available; and whether the funds could be bought online. Tables 10.5 and 10.6 show, in our opinion, the 20 best and 29 worst sites in these respects at the time of writing.

The comments that follow are in two broad sections: websites of fund management groups running government bond (or gilt) funds on the one hand, and the sites of those running corporate bond funds on the other. To some degree they overlap.

Government bond funds

Taking government bond funds first, Aberdeen Asset Management's site (www.aberdeen-asset.com) provides substantial information about its Gilt Income Unit Trust. It lists the key features including charges, gross income yields and gross redemption yields. There is a downloadable fact sheet. It gives information on the top ten holdings, sector breakdown, key features, managers' report and a performance table. The annual and interim reports for the trust can also be downloaded. The fund price, updated daily at noon, is displayed at the site. There is a brief biography of the fund manager. This is an important item, but one omitted at the majority of sites. There is also a link to Trustnet for further information.

By contrast investors interested in Guardian's Gilt and Fixed Interest Fund will find little to whet their appetite at Guardian's website (www.guardianfs.co.uk). The only feature of interest is a link to FT.com for prices. The site's designer says that they welcome questions about the site.

Table 10.5 Funds showing most information on their websites

Name of trust	Management group	Management bios	Fact sheet	Performance data	Buy online
Gilt Income Unit Trust	Aberdeen Asset Managers	Yes	Yes	Yes	No
Aberdeen Global Champions Fund	Aberdeen Asset Managers	Yes	Yes	Yes	No
Fixed Interest Unit Trust	Aberdeen Asset Managers	Yes	Yes	Yes	No
High Yield Bond Unit Trust	Aberdeen Asset Managers	Yes	Yes	Yes	No
Sterling Bond Unit Trust	Aberdeen Asset Managers	Yes	Yes	Yes	No
Gerrard UK Fixed Interest Fund	Gerrard Investment Funds	Yes	Yes	Yes	No
Gerrard International Bond & Convertible Fund	Gerrard Investment Funds	Yes	Yes	Yes	No
Govett Corporate Bond Fund	Govett Investments	Yes	Yes	Yes	No
Corporate Bond Fund	Jupiter Unit Trust Managers	Yes	Yes	Yes	Yes
LeggMason Investors Monthly Income Unit Trust	LeggMason Investors Unit Trust Managers Ltd	Yes	Yes	Yes	No
Murray Corporate Bond Fund	Murray Johnstone Unit Trust Management Ltd	Yes	Yes	Yes	No
Murray Global Bond Fund	Murray Johnstone Unit Trust Management Ltd	Yes	Yes	Yes	No
High Yield Bond Fund	Newton Fund Managers	Yes	Yes	Yes	No
European High Yield Bond Fund	Newton Fund Managers	Yes	Yes	Yes	No
International Bond Fund	Newton Fund Managers	Yes	Yes	Yes	No
Royal & Sun Alliance Maximum Income Bond Fund	Royal & Sun Alliance Investments	Yes	Yes	Yes	Yes
Royal & Sun Alliance High Income Bond Trust	Royal & Sun Alliance Investments	Yes	Yes	Yes	Yes
Royal & Sun Alliance Worldwide Bond Trust	Royal & Sun Alliance Investments	Yes	Yes	Yes	Yes
Preferred Income Trust	Singer & Friedlander	Yes	Yes	Yes	No
S&W Fixed Interest Trust	Smith & Williamson Unit Trust Managers	Yes	Yes	Yes	No

Source: Company websites

Table 10.6 Funds with least information on their websites

Name of trust	Management group	Management bios	Fact sheet	Performance data	Buy online
Gilt Fund	Aberdeen Asset Managers	No	No	No	No
Whittingdale Sterling Bond Fund	ACM Investments	No	No	No	No
S&P High Income Fund	Chase Fleming Asset Management	No	No	No	No
S&P International Bond Fund	Chase Fleming Asset Management	No	No	No	No
City Financial International Capital Accumulator	City Financial Investment company	No	No	No	No
Institutional Long Gilt Fund	Fidelity Investment Services	No	No	No	No
Institutional UK Index Linked Bond Fund	Fidelity Investment Services	No	No	No	No
Institutional International Bond Fund	Fidelity Investment Services	No	No	No	No
Institutional UK Bond Fund	Fidelity Investment Services	No	No	No	No
Select Long Dated Gilt Fund	Fleming Unit Trust Management	No	No	No	No
Select UK Bond Fund	Fleming Unit Trust Management	No	No	No	No
Select UK Index-Linked Bond Fund	Fleming Unit Trust Management	No	No	No	No
Select Global Bond Fund	Fleming Unit Trust Management	No	No	No	No
Gilt & Fixed Interest Trust	Guardian Unit Managers	No	No	No	No
Extra Income Trust	Guardian Unit Managers	No	No	No	No
Corporate Bond Fund	HSBC Investment Funds	No	No	No	No
Merrill Lynch Long Dated Sterling Bcnd# Fund	Merrill Lynch Fund Managers	No	No	No	No
International Bond Trust	MGM Unit Managers	No	No	No	No
Natwest Extra Income Trust	Natwest Unit Trust Managers	No	No	No	No
Higher Income Plus Fund	Norwich Union Investment Funds	No	No	No	No
Shorter Term Securities Exempt	Phillips & Drew Unit Managers	No	No	No	No
High Yield	Royal Bank of Scotland Trust Management	No	No	No	No
Gilt & Fixed Interest Fund	Schroder Unit Trust Limited	No	No	No	No
Mercury Corporate Bond	Scottish Amicable Unit Trust and PEP Managers	No	No	No	No
Corporate Bond Trust	Scottish Widows Fund Management	No	No	No	No
International Bond Trust	Scottish Widows Fund Management	No	No	No	No
Corporate Bond Unit Trust	St James's Place Unit Trust Group	No	No	No	No
Thesis High Income Fund	Thesis Unit Trust Management	No	No	No	No
Corporate Bond Fund	Woolwich Unit Trust Managers	No	No	No	No

Source: Company websites

The site of Guardian's parent company Aegon (www.aegon.co.uk) is also noticeable for its lack of content. It merely provides links to its subsidiaries. To be kind, one could assume that both these sites are still in the development stage, although there is no obvious evidence that this is so.

Framlington's site (www.framlington.co.uk) is easy to navigate and well designed. The opening page on unit trusts has a brief introduction. Other data include the range of funds on offer, a performance chart of all the firm's unit trusts and a downloadable application form. There is a downloadable fact sheet similar to that on offer from Aberdeen Asset Managers. The fund data show cumulative performance over the last ten years and consistency of performance on a half-yearly basis.

The Merrill Lynch web pages devoted to its Government Securities Fund (www.mlim.co.uk) are, like those relating to its other unit trusts, among the most informative. The firm provides an overview of all its trusts together with the key benefits and objectives. In addition there are performance charts for each trust covering the last five years. These include a comparison with the FTSE Gilts All-Stocks Index. It is also possible to view the trust's performance for any period by entering the required dates. The site gives recent unit trust prices, together with a portfolio breakdown and a list of the largest holdings. A downloadable brochure has information on all its unit trust and ISAs. This is also the only site to offer a tool enabling investors to check the latest value of their holdings.

Information on the Whittingdale Gilt Funds is at the site of its parent company, ACM Investments (www.acmfunds.com). The information is sparse – just one page. It does, however, give the top ten holdings, the fund's objective and some performance data. The name of the fund manager is mentioned, but the site provides no other details except for length of tenure.

Still wondering which company to trust with your money? You may find the following descriptions taken from the websites concerned worth taking into account: Framlington 'has never been in better shape'; Aegon is 'robust'; ACM has 'an outstanding record of money management'; and Merrill Lynch is 'the largest'. By contrast, modesty prevails at Aberdeen Asset Management. It doubtless feels no need for superlatives, letting its performance speak for itself.

> **Still wondering which company to trust with your money?**

Corporate bond funds

We look next at the website quality of fund management groups involved in running corporate bond funds. One of the best sites is Royal and Sun

Alliance's (www.rsainvestments.co.uk). The home page has a site map and search facility. It lists each fund with direct links to information giving performance data, a fund's largest holdings, its investment style, a portfolio breakdown, and a biography of the fund manager. This information is also available as a downloadable factsheet. A separate section covers the definition of unit trusts and OEICs together with the advantages of this sort of investment. Daily fund prices can also be found on the site. Another useful section provides answers to key questions such as taxation, bid/offer spreads, and why OEICs are replacing unit trusts. A 'why invest' section of the site covers areas such as risk and reward, security, diversification and the impact of inflation. This is one of the few sites where it is possible to invest online as well as viewing information.

Aberdeen Asset Managers site (www.aberdeen-asset.co.uk) is easy to navigate and informative. There is a direct link from the home page to the section about funds. This seemingly ordinary facility is not provided on many sites, which often makes the information difficult to find. A fund fact sheet similar to that provided by Royal and Sun Alliance can be downloaded, together with interim and annual fund reports. The site provides some general information about the distinction between unit trusts and OEICs.

Chase Fleming (www.chaseflemingam.co.uk) offers online dealing and valuations. The site is detailed. Apart from the usual fund details and per-formance data, there is a monthly commentary from the fund manager and general comments on the investment outlook. There is a monthly overview from the firm's investment director. The 'investor help' section gives advice on which product to choose and ways to invest. Various investor guides can be downloaded.

Another site where it is possible to buy online is Jupiter Unit Trust Managers (www.jupiteronline.co.uk). This is part of Jupiter International Group, now owned by Commerzbank, a German bank. The site gives fund and performance details together with the latest prices.

Newton Fund Managers (www.newton.co.uk) provides performance tables for one, three and five years since the launch of each of its funds. It is also possible to compare these tables with the sector's average. The tables can be downloaded to a spreadsheet. The fund facts are not as detailed as those provided on some other sites, but there are other features. This includes 'portfolio manager', a tool that investors can use to keep track of their Newton fund investments. The site also has an email alert facility, to provide updated fund prices.

Legg Mason Investors (www.leggmason.com) site suffers from a fussy design. Accessing the key features document for each fund requires the use of Microsoft ActiveX Gallery. This has to be downloaded separately.

The site does however provide a 12-page unit trust brochure. This explains the investment procedure and features of its unit trusts. Data on prices and performance are updated daily.

Govett Investments (www.govett.co.uk) also suffers from design anomalies. The site map has no direct links to information. Only the most persistent investors will track down the information they need. Once located, fund facts, performance and reports and accounts are all present on the site. In addition there is an explanatory brochure and prospectus. The search facility on the site failed to return any mention of the firm's own corporate bond fund. This is common at fund websites and Govett is not alone in this respect.

At the time of writing Gerrard was in the process of merging with Capel Cure Sharp and consequently the two firms' websites were being merged and redesigned. Also temporarily unavailable was information on individual funds from Norwich Union and Phillips and Drew. Search facilities at this site were not operating.

In general terms, bank fund management subsidiaries are also particularly coy when it comes to providing easy access to information on their investment funds. Two other sites worthy of a special mention are those of Singer and Friedlander (www.singers.co.uk) and Smith and Williamson (www.smith.williamson.co.uk). The latter provides daily price and performance details courtesy of Trustnet. Both sites include fund facts and performance details.

As with its gilt funds, investors looking for information on corporate bonds at Guardian's site (www.guardianfs.co.uk) will be disappointed. The home page is inviting but further investigation reveals a distinct lack of content. The site may be in the course of redevelopment following the firm's acquisition by Aegon, but Aegon's own site (www.aegon.co.uk) also lacks information. At the time this chapter was written the 'in focus' part of the site was devoid of information but asked users what additional information they would like to find there. The feedback section of the site also asked for comments. The only fund information provided is by way of a third-party link to FT.com.

The Royal Bank of Scotland's site (www.rbs.co.uk) is complicated and provides only limited general information on its funds. MGM Assurance's site is still being developed. No information is available on the MGM International Bond Trust, but there is a downloadable life and pension fund portfolio brochure.

Scottish Amicable's (www.scottishamicable.co.uk) site was gimmicky. It uses fictional examples – a recent university graduate and a well-paid professional manager in a large company – to demonstrate investors' fund needs. The site claims to offer a huge amount of information, but it is hard to locate. Little of substance appears to be available, other than a brief description of the funds. Further information can be obtained on request. Prices can be found through a link to FT.com.

IN BRIEF

- Many investors use unit trusts and other similar vehicles to invest in bonds.

- Collective investments like these allow investors to spread risk, gain the expertise of a professional fund and have a diversified portfolio.

- ISAs allow UK investors to compound investment returns free of tax. This can be valuable for investors reinvesting income from high-yielding funds.

- Investors in bond funds often incur charges. It may be worth opting for a fund even if it has high charges, if it has a particularly strong performance record.

- Charges can sometimes be minimized by buying through a fund supermarket.

- Investors in corporate bond funds should look beyond the fund's headline yield at information on the underlying portfolio. Many bond funds have generated high yields only by putting investors capital at greater risk.

- There is a considerable amount of fund data available on the web, both at independent sites like Trustnet and at fund management groups' own websites.

- Fund management groups' websites vary considerable in the quality of information they provide.

Afterword: where bond markets go from here

Astute investors are flexible. They recognize that the investments which have served them well in the recent past may not be the ones that are appropriate in the future. So it may pay investors to look now and in the future at the combination of

risk and reward that bonds offer. No one disputes that in the long term shares provide the best returns. But higher returns do not come without higher risks attached and we may have to wait for the long term for those returns to arrive. As John Maynard Keynes said, 'In the long run, we are all dead.'

If shares are often the best performers, bonds provide their best returns only under certain circumstances. Those circumstances are benign inflation, falling corporate profits and a climate of fear in the share markets. They are the conditions ruling at present in the markets. At the time of writing there were plenty of reasons for believing that share markets were still substantially overvalued. If the historical relationships that have held good in previous downswings in the stock market cycle are to hold good again (and why shouldn't they?) then returns from bond investments may be better than those from shares for some time to come, even though they have generated good performance already.

The long bear market in Japanese equities is often held to be a special case that derives from the unique nature of Japanese financial institutions and government. But the fact remains that the bubble in the US stock market has yet to be fully deflated and there are plenty of signs of corporate excess that still need to be purged from the system before things can return to normal. The US Federal Reserve has chosen to use lower interest rates as an aggressive weapon of policy, cutting rates to try and revive confidence. But confidence in the US economy is fragile and the logic of the moves suggest that interest rates could fall substantially further from current levels, boosting bond prices. Bond yields in Japan, where short-term interest rates are close to zero, are between 1% and 2%.

In my view, this is the ideal time to accept the certainty that the bond markets offer. As previous chapters have demonstrated you can more than likely use your existing broker to deal in bonds. You can buy bonds online. If you buy most government bonds and hold them to maturity you have guaranteed returns, with no risk and only limited price volatility. You can buy bonds with an equity kicker, bonds that are tax efficient, bonds that are inflation proofed, and many other variants.

Corporate bond funds offer a way of accessing higher yields while limiting risk through diversification, but the higher risk end of this spectrum needs to be avoided for the time being. Default rates on corporate bonds are increasing and could rise much further in the next year or so, particularly in the USA. Defaulting on a bond remains a last resort for a company, but by no means an unknown one, while credit rating downgrades are commonplace.

This is the ideal time to accept the certainty that the bond markets offer.

On the horizon, so-called exchange traded funds, which can be dealt in like shares but mimic the performance of an index, have ultra-low charges (unlike index tracking unit trusts). ETFs like this are being constructed to mimic bond indices just as they are currently available for equity markets. Products like this will open up the bond market even further and perhaps lead investors to take a more rounded view of their investments, allocating assets in a sensible way rather than simply buying shares on the basis of hunches and ill-considered momentum.

More sophisticated asset allocation, lower inflation, lower – or negative – returns from shares for some time to come and a lower propensity to accept risk are likely to encourage investors to look more closely at bonds. And not before time. I hope this book has helped the readers to get to grips with bonds and what they can offer to sensible and thoughtful investors.

Appendix 1 Glossary

Accrued interest Interest that has been earned on a bond since its last interest payment date. When a bond is sold, the seller receives accrued interest from the buyer.

Basis point One-hundredth of 1 per cent. Basis points are commonly used to measure difference between bond yields.

Bearer bonds Bonds that are not registered and assumed to be the property of those presenting them.

Benchmark A bond against whose yield other bonds are measured.

BOBL A type of German government bond.

BTF A type of French government bond.

BTP A type of Italian government bond.

Bulldog bond A bond issued in sterling and marketed to UK investors by a non-British issuer.

Bullet A bond that repays principal in full in a single payment on redemption.

Bund A type of German government bond.

BUXL A type of German government bond.

Callable bond A bond where, under certain circumstances and on pre-set terms, the issuer has the option to buy back the bond from holders.

Clean price The price of a bond excluding accrued interest. Bond prices are always quoted 'clean', unless stated otherwise.

Convergence The tendency of the yields of a group of bonds to move towards a common benchmark.

Convertible bond A bond that contains an inbuilt option to exchange it for shares in the issuer.

Corporate bond A bond issued by a company rather than the government.

Coupon The annual rate of interest paid on a bond.

Credit rating An objective measure of an issuer's creditworthiness. The credit rating affects the price and yield on which the issuer's bonds stand.

CREST An electronic settlement system for UK shares, bonds and other securities.

Debentures Bonds secured against specific assets, usually property.

Default The failure of an issuer to pay interest in full or on time, or to repay principal in full or on time.

Deflation A period of falling consumer prices, the opposite of inflation.

Discounting Adjusting future cash flows, such as interest payments, to reflect investors' preference for receiving cash sooner rather than later.

Distressed debt Bonds that have defaulted or are widely expected to default.

Duration The average life of a bond as measured by its discounted cash flows.

EURIBOR Euro InterBank Offered Rate – a benchmark short-term interest rate for the Euro-zone.

Eurobonds Bonds issued and sold to investors outside the country whose currency is used.

Eurocurrencies Money deposited by companies and governments in banks outside their home country.

Exchangeable bond A bond that contains an inbuilt option to exchange it for shares in a company other than the issuer.

Floating rate notes Bonds whose interest rate is tied to a reference rate such as LIBOR or EURIBOR.

GEMMs Gilt-edge market makers.

Gilt-edge stock Nickname for British government bonds.

Government bonds Bonds issued by a sovereign government. Bonds issued by governments in OECD countries and Japan are deemed free from risk of default.

Index-linked bonds Bonds whose face value and interest payments are linked to the retail price index and which therefore offer an inflation protected return.

Inverse floaters Bonds whose interest payments vary inversely to a reference rate such as LIBOR or EURIBOR.

ISMA International Securities Market Association, a trade association for the Eurobond market.

JGB Japanese government bond.

Junk bonds Bonds whose issuers lack a credit rating or whose credit quality is deemed below 'investment grade'; sometimes called 'high-yield bonds'.

LIBOR London InterBank Offered Rate – a benchmark short-term interest rate.

Nominal value The face value of a bond, as distinct from the amount an investor might have paid for it.

OAT A type of French government bond.

OEIC An open-ended investment company, equivalent to a unit trust or mutual fund.

Pfandebriefe A bond issued by a German mortgage bank and carrying a government guarantee.

Portfolio A group of investments held by a fund or an individual investor.

Primary market The market for new issues of bonds and other securities.

Prior charge A claim that a bond may have on the assets of a company ahead of other securities, in the event of liquidation.

Puttable bonds Bonds that allow the holder, under certain circum-stances and on pre-set terms, to sell the bonds back to the issuer.

Redemption date (maturity date) The date on which a bond's principal amount is repaid.

Redemption yield The annual percentage return received by an investor if the bond is held from purchase to maturity; a universally used system for comparing bonds.

Repo (repurchase agreement) market A system through which market professionals make and receive collateralized loans backed by bonds and cash.

Running yield A bond's coupon expressed as a percentage of its price.

Samurai bond A bond issued in yen to Japanese investors by a non-Japanese issuer.

Secondary market. The day-to-day market used by investors to buy and sell bonds and other securities once issued.

Senior debt Bonds that rank ahead of all other debt for repayment in the event of liquidation. Outranked only by debentures secured on specific assets.

Sinking fund bonds Bonds that repay a portion of principal each year instead of on a single maturity date.

Spread The difference between two bond yields, usually between a bond yield and a recognized benchmark yield. Usually displayed in basis points.

STRIPS Separate Trading of Registered Interest and Principal of Securities. The mechanism used to create zero-coupon bonds.

Subordinated (junior) debt Bonds whose claims rank behind debentures and senior debt in the event of a corporate liquidation.

Swap curve A benchmark yield curve inferred from swaps transactions and the related credit rating of the issuers involved.

Swaps Transactions conducted through investment banks in which bond issuers exchange fixed rate liabilities for floating ones (and vice versa).

Ticker symbols Short three- or four-letter codes that designate particular bonds or stocks. Used to call up prices or in online dealing.

Time value of money The universal human preference for receiving cash sooner rather than later. It is the reason why yields on longer dated bonds should be higher than shorter dated ones. Used as the basis for discounting future interest payments.

Tombstones Advertisements placed by managers of bond issues to publicize their role in arranging an issue.

Total return The combination of the annual income yielded by an investment, plus or minus any capital gain or loss, expressed as a percentage of the cost of that investment.

Undated (or irredeemable) bonds Bonds that have no redemption date.

Underwriting syndicate An informal group of banks set up to market a bond issue to investors, with one bank acting as 'lead manager'.

Unsecured debt Debt whose claim for repayment ranks after all other forms of debt securities in the event of a corporate liquidation.

Volatility A statistical measure of the degree to which an investment fluctuates in price. Often used as a proxy for risk.

Yankee bond A bond issued in dollars to American investors by a non-US issuer.

Yield curve A graph plotting the redemption yields on bonds in order of their redemption date.

Zero-coupon bonds Bonds which carry no coupon and whose return derives from the fact that they are sold at a significant discount to their eventual redemption value.

Appendix 2 Bond-related websites

Company	Web address	Category
Aberdeen Asset Management	www.aberdeen-asset.com	Funds
ACM Investments	www.acmfunds.com	Funds
ADVFN	www.advfn.com	Portal
Aegon	www.aegon.co.uk	Funds
APCIMS	www.apcims.co.uk	Brokers
Bank of England	www.bankofengland.co.uk	Govt
Bank of Japan	www.boj.or.jp/en/	Govt
Barclays Capital	www.barclayscapital.com	Inv. Bank
Bloomberg	www.bloomberg.co.uk	Portal
Bond Resources	www.bondresources.com	General
Bureau of Public Debt	www.publicdebt.treas.gov	Govt
Business Week	www.businessweekeurope.com	News
Calculatorweb	www.calculatorweb.com/	Calculator
CBOT	www.cbot.com	Futures
CME	www.cme.com	Futures
CNet Download.com	www.download.com	Software
Compoundit!	www.bondsonline.com	Calculator
Debt Management Office	www.dmo.gov.uk	Govt
Dismal Scientist	www.dismal.com	Economics
Egg	www.egg.com	Funds
Eurex	www.eurexchange.com	Futures
European Central Bank	www.ecb.int	Govt
Federal Reserve	www.federalreserve.gov	Govt
Fidelity	www.fundsdirect.co.uk	Funds
Financecenter	www.financecenter.com	Calculator
Fitch	www.fitch.com	Ratings
Forbes	www.forbes.com	News
Framlington	www.framlington.co.uk	Funds
FT.com	www.ft.com	News
FTmarketwatch	www.ftmarketwatch.com	Prices
Govett Investments	www.govett.co.uk	Funds
Guardian	www.guardianfs.co.uk	Funds
HM Treasury	www.hm-treasury.gov.uk	Govt

Indexfunds.com	www.indexfunds.com	ETFs
Interactive Investor	www.iii.co.uk	Portal
Intermoney	www.intermoney.com	Economics
Investing in Bonds	www.investinginbonds.com	General
Investors Chronicle	www.investorschronicle.co.uk	News
iShares	www.ishares.com	ETFs
Japanese Ministry of Finance	www.mof.go.jp	Govt
JP Morgan	www.jpmorgan.com	Inv. Bank
Kauders Portfolio Management	www.gilt.co.uk	General
Kiplingers	www.kiplinger.com	News
Legg Mason	www.leggmason.com	Funds
LIFFE	www.liffe.com	Futures
Lombard Street Research	www.lombard-st.co.uk	Economics
Long Bond	www.longbond.com	General
Merrill Lynch	www.mlim.co.uk	Funds
Moody's	www.moodys.com	Ratings
Newslink	www.ajr.org	News
Office of National Statistics	www.statistics.gov.uk	Stats
Quote.com	www.quote.com	Prices
Reuters Credit	http://credit.reuters.com	Portal
Reuters	http://quotes.reuters.com	Prices
Riskgrades	www.riskgrades.com	Risk
Royal Bank of Scotland	www.rbs.co.uk	Funds
Royal Sun Alliance	www.rsainvestments.co.uk	Funds
Scottish Amicable	www.scottishamicable.co.uk	Funds
Singer and Friedlander	www.singers.co.uk	Funds
Smith and Williamson	www.smith.williamson.co.uk	Funds
Standard & Poors	www.standardpoor.com	Funds
Technical University	www.ntu.edu.sg/library/statdata.htm	Funds
The Economist	www.economist.com	News
US Census Bureau	www.census.gov/main/	Stats
Wall Street Journal	www.wsj.com	News
Yardeni Economic Network	www.yardeni.com	Economics

Appendix 3 Further reading

Title	Author(s)	Publisher
Dictionary of Finance & Investment	Downes and Goodman	Barrons
French Financial Markets	Durieux, Serieyssol, Stephan	Gresham
Getting Started in Bonds	Michael Thomsett	John Wiley
Guide to World Bond Markets	Essex and Pitchford	John Wiley
International Financial Markets	J Orlin Grabbe	Prentice Hall
Introduction to Bond Markets	Reuters/Financial Training	John Wiley
Introduction to FX and Money Mkts	Reuters/Financial Training	John Wiley
Introduction to International Money Markets	Keith Redhead	Woodhead-Faulkner
Inventing Money	Nicholas Dunbar	John Wiley
The Bond Book	Annette Thau	McGraw Hill
The Euro	Paul Temperton (ed.)	John Wiley
The Eurobond Diaries	Shearlock and Ellington	Euroclear
The Ratings Game	Andrew Fight	John Wiley

Index